Cal

The true
English nurse and her work
with the Paumarí

To Christine,

Best wishes & every blessing,

Shirley Chapman.

by Margaret Gee
with Shirley Chapman

Lastword Publications
Lowestoft, Suffolk, UK
www.lastwordpublications.com

First published 2012, by Lastword Publications
www.lastwordpublications.com
Lastword Publications works with authors and musicians, businesses and charities to provide professional results with maximum impact.

ISBN 978 0 9559439 7 3

The publishers wish to express their gratitude to the following for permission to include copyright material in this book.

Scripture quotations taken from the Amplified® Bible, Copyright © 1954, 1958, 1962, 1964, 1965, 1987 by The Lockman Foundation. Used by permission. www. Lockman.org

The Holy Bible, New International Version®, NIV® Copyright © 1973, 1978, 1984, 2011 by Biblica, Inc.™ Used by permission. All rights reserved worldwide.

Scripture taken from the New King James Version. Copyright © 1982 by Thomas Nelson. Inc. Used by permission. All rights reserved.

Scripture quotations marked (NLT) are taken from the Holy Bible, New Living Translation, copyright © 1996, 2004, 2007 by Tyndale House Foundation. Used by permission of Tyndale House Publishers, Inc., Carol Stream, Illinois 60188. All rights reserved.

Scripture taken from The Message. Copyright © 1993, 1994, 1995, 1996, 2000, 2001, 2002. Used by permission of NavPress Publishing Group.

Design and production by The Upper Room (London, UK) 020 8406 1010
The front cover image is from a painting by Meinke Salzer

'*The people who sat in darkness have seen a great Light, and for those who sat in the land and shadow of death Light has dawned.*' (Matthew 4:16)

'Bakibakiki fori hiki ida vakadiarabo vavaibaviki.
Hari. Vanokiki bana ida vagani fori hiki karaho.
Vagahahaviki bana ida vaibavi.
Va'ora navagaki bana adani ija'ari vaabiniki fori vihiki.
Ni-Deu-ra avigariha adani.'

Deceased Isaiah wrote in God's word paper. He spoke ahead of time about the place where Jesus would travel around before His word came to pass. (Literal translation of Matthew 4:14)

Nimania ida Deus athi kapapirani Isaías kohana binajiri'iki. Isaías kohana vara bivani'a'bo'da'iki hihida vaibavia Jesus aadahaonina, oniani ida kidivarani nanamithani hi'ia.'
(in Paumarí)

This book is dedicated to the glory of God and to the power of His Word.

It honours the life and devotion of Shirley Chapman who spent more than thirty years with a remote indigenous group of people in the Amazon jungle. Shirley followed God's call to live and work with the Paumarí people, learning their unwritten language, devising a way to write it, teaching them to read and then working to translate the scriptures for them.

It also honours the partnership with Mary Ann Odmark who worked with Shirley for many years, and Meinke Salzer who joined them in 1976 and who, with Shirley, saw it to its completion.

Many other people around the world have dedicated their life's work to the translation of the scriptures. Countless others still do. We honour them all.

Each language has some special and useful feature which the explorer of language, the linguist, has the privilege of finding, like a seam of gold running through a rock.

One feature that is particularly useful in the Paumarí language is the acceptability of saying 'Shirley (they)', a singular noun followed by a plural verb. As Margaret has written this book and named just a few people, it may appear that we were the only ones involved. In fact, in most of the stories, there are many unnamed people without whom the events would not have occurred. These unnamed people – nurses and patients, translators and consultants, pilots and directors, the list is endless – are the background 'they' to this story.

As this story has been told it has been our desire that Jesus, though often unnamed, be recognised as the constant participant throughout. It was He who instigated it, choosing a rather timid and not highly educated young lady, and sending her off to a remote place in the Amazon rainforest, just because He wanted to give the Paumarí people a chance to hear that He loved them and wanted to help them. It was a task that was far too big for her to accomplish alone, so He put in place a very great number of people to accompany her in this task. Most of these tried to help and facilitate the goal of getting that message to the Paumarí. 'They' are the brightly coloured threads which He has woven into this story. Some have been darker threads, trying to hinder or impede. Thank God for the light and the dark threads without which there would have been no background design to the story you are about to read. So, 'Shirley (they)...'

Shirley Chapman

During the years when Shirley lived and worked in Brazil, certain words were used in everyday language. Some of them are now deemed unacceptable and I have tried to respect that. It was particularly hard to refrain from using the word 'tribe'. In addition, members of indigenous groups were often called 'Indians', and most other people 'Brazilians'. Both of these terms have been altered unless there was very good reason not to do so.

Margaret Gee

Fátima with a baby sloth

Contents

Foreword

Often when I watch the news on television, I admire the reporters who leave the comfort of their homes and travel to foreign lands in the hunt for 'breaking news' to send back to their broadcasting organisations.

For some, in the front line of war or uprisings, their role often looks extremely dangerous. What motivates them to leave families and the comparative security and comfort of life at home, to be there as presidents fall and missiles fly? Perhaps there is the thrill of adventure, a sense of pride in being the first to report back, or maybe it is simply a means of earning a living wage. They hope to send news back, but what do they have to take with them?

The Bible gives accounts of many people who lived life on the front line. They had responded to the call of God and, as a result, experienced dangerous ventures. Some were exciting, most were costly, and few, if any, resulted in a large bank balance! A number even gave their lives in the ultimate sacrifice.

Many of the developments the world has seen and enjoy today have been as a result of the hard work and tears of men and women called to serve by the God of the universe.

Such was the call on Shirley's life. As a young girl, what on earth was going on in her mind to lead her to the Amazon Jungle, to live there with an unknown group of people, to learn an unwritten language and to sacrifice all her life in serving them? What light was shining in Shirley's heart that eliminated the thick darkness of the Amazon Jungle?

Well, I believe that unlike journalists, Shirley had Good News to bring to the people, one of whom she was now to become. She knew that there is a greater sacrifice that was given for her, and all she could do was to give some of the people in the Amazon Jungle a chance to hear the news about the salvation of the humankind.

Our God is still in the business of sending people out to advance His purposes. There is no greater calling. I thank God that because of people who gave their all and responded to the call just like Shirley did, today I can read the Word of God in my mother tongue and understand the will of God for my life.

Georges Kisombola

Glossary

FUNAI	Fundação Nacional do Índio (National Indian Foundation)
JAARS	Jungle and Aviation Radio Service
LBC	London Bible College
MAF	Missionary Aviation Fellowship
Mimeograph	otherwise known as a duplicator
Shaman	otherwise known as a witch-doctor
SIL	Summer Institute of Linguistics
WBT	Wycliffe Bible Translators

1 Grief

She panted hard as she cycled along, willing her legs to move faster. She knew that it was a race against time. Her heart was pounding in her chest, and sobs rose in her throat as she leaned further over the handle bars. She leapt off her bike at the doctor's house and pounded on the door. She waited a moment and then knocked again, harder this time and with unmistakable urgency. The door remained shut.

It was then that she saw the notice. 'The surgery is closed on Thursday afternoons. In an emergency you will need to telephone this number.' She had no money with her and had never used a telephone in her life. Neither did she have any paper or a pencil to write down the information from the notice. But there was no time to lose. She said the number over to herself a few times and then, as she got back on her bicycle, she kept repeating it over and over, until it began to sound like a drum beat in her head. She cycled back home as fast as she could and rushed in, gasping out the message to her father. They did not have a phone at home and she would have to go back and use the one in the phone box on the corner. He quickly found the four pennies which she would need and hastily gave her some instructions on how to use the public phone.

She had barely got her breath back but climbed on her bike once more and set off again. She was grateful to find that the phone box was empty. She picked up the receiver and with trembling fingers, dialled the number. The doctor himself answered and she fed the pennies in one by one. She was shaking so much and thought that she would drop them, but finally managed it and then pressed hard on Button A to get the connection. It was such a stiff button and her fingers now felt so weak. She was hardly coherent as she blurted out the message. Her mother had collapsed at the table during lunch.

Please could he come? Her voice was breaking with sobs. The doctor told her that he would be on his way immediately.

Her head was spinning as she cycled home again, thinking back to the time when her mother had first suffered a stroke. Shirley was only eight years old then, and her mother was just 38. She was too young to understand the full implications of someone having had a stroke. All she knew was that her mother could not speak properly and it was hard to understand her. She was partially paralysed but had gradually learned to walk again with the help of a stick. She had tried to do some exercises to build up her strength, but it was war time and there was no expert help available. But to Shirley she was mum; her mum, someone who loved her unconditionally, and whose life now hung in the balance.

It was the early 1940s and Britain was still embroiled in World War II. Home was in Ilford, on the border of Essex and the East End of London. Although nowhere was safe, the East End was a particularly vulnerable place to live. War time was so unsettling, and there had already been various times of evacuation. Before their mother had been ill the first time she herself had taken both children to live in Bristol. After a while, however, nothing dramatic seemed to be happening in London and so they returned to the family home. Later on, the whole school was evacuated to Somerset. Shirley and her older brother Peter were placed together in a family home. It was a strange time, both for the evacuees but also for those who were suddenly expected to care for bewildered and frightened children.

When Shirley and Peter were fed on nothing but chips and doughnuts, not only did it soon become very monotonous but they also quickly developed skin infections. When their parents came to visit one day the host family gave them a proper meal, but a chance remark alerted their father to the reality of their life there, and he decided to take them home immediately. Lessons then continued around the dining room table, with other children joining them until the local school was able to reopen.

Memories tumbled through Shirley's mind that Thursday afternoon. Her breath was now coming in gulping sobs and her stomach seemed to have got tied in a knot. She was so frightened. As she arrived back home she was immediately ushered into a neighbour's house. Someone gave her a drink of water and a handkerchief. She was grateful for the drink but then sat silently, twisting the hankie nervously in her lap.

She was not sure how much time passed but she heard someone come to the front door. There were hushed voices and then she was aware that her father had come into the room. She did not dare look up into his face but as he sat down, her heart skipped a beat. He could hardly speak, and afterwards she could not remember what he had said. But she knew the reason well enough. He had come to tell her that her mother had suffered a second stroke. At just 39, she was dead.

Peter was not there that afternoon. He had been evacuated once again, this time further out of London to the county of Norfolk, with their grandmother. Someone arranged for a telegram to be sent to her and she brought Peter home later in the day. Shirley had turned 10 years old, Peter was 12. They were totally devastated – and wept together.

In the days that followed various people helped out. An auntie had already been doing some of the washing and she was there for some of the time. Neighbours did what they could. No one seemed to know what to say to the children and they were largely left alone. The time passed in a blur, but when the day of the funeral arrived the children were not allowed to go. Grief and loneliness swept over Shirley and she felt as though her heart would break.

The house seemed so empty. Although their mother had not been able to speak much for some time, she had been there to welcome them when they came home from school. Now it just seemed to echo with emptiness. As days became weeks and the weeks turned into months, a new and strange feeling seemed to take over inside Shirley. Anger had begun to rise in her and tormented her wherever she went. She was angry with God in particular and demanded that He give her back her mother.

Their father, Sydney, was a sick man himself. He had a longstanding problem with tuberculosis (TB) and as a result, had not been called up to serve in the war. He had been a radio operator in the merchant navy for some years, but had left it when Peter was born. At times he spent many weeks in bed. Pleurisy often complicated his recovery and sometimes when the family doctor came to visit, he would remove large quantities of fluid from Sydney's chest to help his breathing. The doctor often did not seem to have a receptacle in which to collect the fluid and Shirley recalled how he would tip the water out of a vase of flowers and use that instead!

When Sydney was well enough he worked as an insurance agent. He also helped out with the Home Guard, dealing with incendiary bombs. Now, however, he was overwhelmed. In addition to his own grief and frailty, he hardly knew how to cope with the two children. He decided that Peter should go to boarding school, but he felt that Shirley was more use at home. So the siblings then lost each other's company and Shirley became a latchkey kid, letting herself in alone when she came home from school. Those moments were particularly lonely. She did what cooking she could and generally helped around the house. Sydney was often out in the evenings as his insurance work meant that he had to visit people at home to collect their premiums. Although there was always plenty for them both to do, they each had to cope with their own grief in their own way.

The war continued and often during the day everyone made frequent trips to the nearest air raid shelter. For some time the family slept in a shelter which had been dug at the end of the garden. Eventually, it became waterlogged and totally useless. A large steel table in the house served as protection during an air raid. A bomb fell into the hole of a neighbour's deserted shelter, doing serious damage to several houses, but no one was killed. If the garden shelters had still been in use there would probably have been many deaths.

It seemed no time at all when Sydney introduced another woman into the household. Her name was Lil. He had decided that the children needed a mother, and that marrying again was the best way to solve the problem. The children were shocked. Memories of their own mother were still too raw, and it was impossible for them to accept this new woman. They refused to call her 'mother' and gave her a really hard time. Lil suffered from rheumatoid arthritis, although when she first came to live with them it was fairly mild.

A visit to church

It was around this time that Shirley became friends with a girl who went to the Cranbrook Baptist Church, in Ilford. Pam invited her to spend the day with their family. Sydney and Lil were going to visit Peter at boarding school, and Shirley was glad to accept the invitation. It was a relief to spend some time in a normal family atmosphere and she started to go to church with them regularly. She was finding friendship at the church and enjoyed that too.

In some ways it was strange to be in church. Although three years had passed since her mother's death, there was still so much anger in her towards God, but at the same time she was learning to enjoy singing about His love. As they sang one day she began to experience a feeling she had not known before. The words of an old hymn touched her deeply.

"And there between us stands the cross, two arms outstretched to save,
A watchman set to guard the way, from that eternal grave." [1]

[1] *From the hymn "Beneath the cross of Jesus', by Elizabeth Cecelia Douglas Clephane (1830 – 1869)*

She knew that something strange was happening inside her. She did not understand the feeling and yet she knew it was real. The minister was inviting people to go to the vestry and commit their lives to God. She really wanted to go, but courage failed her. Just then Pam leaned over and whispered in her ear. "Would you like to go?"

Shirley gave a small nod and Pam got up immediately to go with her. As Shirley returned to her seat some time later she knew that God had touched her. She could not explain it, but she could feel His love in a way that she had never experienced before. She understood for the first time that He *really did* love her. She had shaken her fist at Him so many times, but now she felt His love. She knew that her hand was no longer clenched in anger but was now open to receive what He had for her. The agony which had tormented her for so long seemed to have melted away, and she felt peace and calm inside. It was hard to believe that it could have happened in just those few minutes, but she knew that it had. Those moments were so special, and she knew that they were life changing. She knew too, that her future was now surrendered to God.

Although in days to come Shirley would look back and know that God's hand had been on her all through her life leading her to that moment, little did she realise that afternoon, that it was also the first step in an amazing journey.

In the days that followed, Shirley realised that she felt differently about Lil. Slowly but surely, she began to see Lil as God's replacement for her mother, and they started to establish a friendship. But it was not an easy atmosphere at home. Sydney and Lil did not really get on well together.

Lil's rheumatoid arthritis had begun to deteriorate and she suffered so much pain. Shirley began to spend hours rubbing her and trying to ease her suffering. Lil had one of the early hip replacement operations and walked for a short time after that, although she gradually became dependent on a wheelchair.

Shirley had passed the 11 plus exam and had gone to the Girls' County High School. It had been her dream to be a vet, but there were no funds available and she knew that it would never be a reality. She was, however, sure about two things: one was that she most definitely did not want to work in an office, and neither did she want to be a nurse.

The school, however, organised interviews for their students, and as a result, Shirley was offered work with *Shell* as a filing clerk. She was just 16 years old. Later on, the father of one of her friends at church obtained a better job for her at the company where he worked in Great Portland Street. The work was more interesting and the pay was higher, but Shirley was restless. There was a question in her spirit which would not go away. She now needed to know what God wanted her to do with her life. She knew that what she wanted was no longer the issue. It was another moment of surrender.

Although she was still quite young, there had already been plenty of challenging experiences in life, and to the casual observer it might have seemed as though Shirley could cope with whatever came along. Inwardly, however, she was quite shy and even rather nervous of meeting new people. It was the youth leaders at the church, Dick and Phyllis Fry, who took a real interest in her, and helped to build up her confidence. Dick gently but firmly encouraged her to start slowly, reading a passage of scripture, leading a prayer, giving out leaflets and talking to people at their doors. One day he asked Shirley to lead a debate. She was panic stricken. She could prepare the first part in advance, but after that, she would have to think on her feet. She felt totally inadequate, but prayed a desperate prayer to God. If He wanted her to do it, then He would have to give her the ability to do so. She added that if He did not, then she would never, ever speak again! God met the challenge and, as a result, the ability to speak in public and lead discussions began to emerge.

From time to time Shirley heard people at the church talk about hearing God speak to them. How did they know it was God, she wondered? Did they actually hear a voice? It was all a bit mysterious. She knew that some of the thoughts which came to her mind were just her own thinking, but over time she began to recognise that others were different. Some of the ideas were things which she knew she would never normally have had. She gradually started to separate her own thoughts from that of God's impressions into her mind, and she began to understand more clearly what other people meant when they said that they could hear God speak.

At other times she might wonder what to do about a particular situation, and then find that some words from a hymn or something that she was reading almost seemed to jump off the page, giving her the answer. Sometimes what appeared to be the most ordinary of things, either in everyday life or in nature, seemed to explain something that she had been wondering about, or brought the answer to a prayer. It might not have meant anything to someone else, but it 'spoke' to her. From time to time she would be listening to someone speak and realise that although it was their voice which she heard, God was using one of His people to speak directly to her.

So it was that in many different ways, she began to recognise that God was indeed 'speaking' to her. It was not a business relationship which they had, but something unique and personal. Just as new friends took time to get to know and trust each other, the relationship was deepening and she was gradually learning to recognise God's 'voice'.

She had asked God what He wanted her to do with her life, and she felt a real conviction about the answer. He was telling her to leave her job and train as a nurse, with a view to being a missionary. At one time, she would have been horrified at the idea, but now she found that she was actually rather excited. She began to dream of distant lands! Dick and Phyllis listened to her vision and encouraged her in it, believing that the call was for real and that God would give her all the gifting she would need.

When she was with them, her faith was encouraged, but at home, it was different. Her father was chronically sick and Lil was in a wheelchair. A home help came to do some of the chores, but Shirley did the washing and the shopping. How could she possibly walk out on them?

Shirley decided to speak to the minister at the church about her dilemma. He offered to meet with Sydney and discuss the situation, but it only seemed to make matters worse. Her father was angry, feeling that she had been influenced by people at the church. He wrote a sharp letter to the minister, and blankly refused to speak to Shirley for a couple of weeks. The atmosphere at home was tense.

Shirley felt torn. On the one hand she read the scripture in her Bible which said "For God commanded, Honor your father and your mother;" [2] On the other hand, she read Jesus' words, "He who loves father and mother more than Me is not worthy of Me". [3] What was the right thing to do? She felt confused and alone.

One morning she was reading the story of Abraham,[4] and of the time when he knew in his heart that God had called him to leave his home and everything he knew. She could imagine him going home to his wife and telling her the news.

"But...but...where are we going?" she could imagine Sarah might have asked.

"I don't know," Abraham replied thoughtfully.

"Well, how long are we going for?" Sarah tried again to get some idea of what this trip was all about.

---

[2] *Matthew 15:4a New King James Version (NKJV)*
[3] *Matthew 10: 37a (NKJV)*
[4] *General thoughts from Genesis 12:1-7*

"I... I... don't know. God did not tell me." Abraham shifted slightly, embarrassed to be pressed for details he did not know.

"Well, for goodness sake," Sarah was now close to tears, but was angry and frustrated at the same time, "Surely you must know *something*".

Shirley felt an affinity with Abraham, called to go somewhere, but not knowing where, why or for how long. She read his story over and over, letting the truth of its words soak into her being, until the moment came when she knew her answer. Like Abraham, she would leave home and all its apparent responsibilities, trusting them into God's care. Like Abraham, she would follow the call of God that was in her heart and, like him she would go, not knowing any more than that.

Shirley began her training at the *Royal London Hospital*, Whitechapel, (formerly *The London Hospital*) in London's East End. Soon after, however, her father was admitted to the annexe of that same hospital which was situated out in Essex. His lungs were badly damaged by TB, and he continued to have recurrent active infections. He needed serious and extensive surgery. For a while Shirley was transferred to the annexe so that she could be near him. She was not on his ward but could, nevertheless, pop in at the end of a shift to see him without having a long journey there and back. It was during these visits that father and daughter began to communicate with each other as adults, and to establish a different relationship. They began to see each other in a new way.

Lil, however, was very frightened. Home alone, apart from carers and neighbours, she urged Shirley to give up her ideas of nursing. But Shirley was now determined to follow God's call. She went home one and a half days a week to do what she could, and a couple of friends from the church also got involved with some of the chores.

One day when she was visiting her father, Sydney turned to look her in the eye. "Does Lil ever say anything to you about giving up nursing?"

"Well, she has mentioned it," Shirley replied casually, hardly daring to say that her step-mother nearly drove her silly with nagging.

"Leave it to me. I will speak to her," Sydney spoke gently. Lil never again asked her to give up her nursing training.

One night when Shirley was on duty in a medical ward, they had a patient who was suffering from advanced skin cancer. The lady was in a serious condition and although it was not her fault, she smelt terrible. The day staff had covered her with a charcoal blanket in a desperate attempt to absorb some of the stench which came from her wounds.

The other nurse on duty with Shirley refused to go near the poor lady, and Shirley was left to change the sheets and tend to the dressings on her own. She was muttering to herself about the unfairness of it all. If her colleague helped her as she was supposed to do, then they could get the job done more quickly and get away from the bed. It would mean less suffering for the patient too. The stench almost made her sick. Just then she felt the nudge of God's spirit and a voice that she had come to recognise. It was as though Jesus Himself was speaking to her.

"Imagine that you are caring for Me," He said. "If I was your patient, how would you feel then?"

In an instant her whole attitude changed and she was able to forgive her colleague and to treat the lady with complete devotion and compassion. As she thought about it later, she reflected how amazing it was that God could change her attitude to a situation in a split second of time if she was willing to let Him do it. It was another moment of surrender, and one which was to have a life-long effect on her.

Time passed and Sydney improved enough to return home. Lil, however, continued to deteriorate and it was felt necessary for her to have a second hip replacement. She was admitted to hospital for surgery. However, before the operation could take place Lil's spinal column suddenly collapsed and she became quadriplegic. It was such a shock for everyone. For Sydney, still a comparatively young man, he was struggling with chronic and very serious health issues himself. He had already lost one young wife and now Lil was totally helpless.

Despite also being relatively young, the only long term bed to be found for Lil was in a geriatric ward. It was a desolate and hopeless life for her, and a huge commitment for the family to support her and visit, none of them knowing for how long it would last.

Shirley and dad, Sydney, 1961

2 Tin kettles

It was already dark outside as Shirley hurried up the dimly lit stairs to the woman's bedroom. The gas light flickered as she entered, and seemed as though it might go out at any moment. As her eyes adjusted to the gloom, she quickly looked around and her heart sank.

She had visited the family a while before to see if the premises were suitable for the mother to give birth at home. It was the 1950s and Britain was still recovering from the war years. Many people were struggling, and the East End of London had its own grinding poverty. On that earlier visit she had discovered that the room had one single bed, plus a double mattress which was on the floor. The door of the room was hanging off its hinges.

"You really must get your husband to fix that door before the baby is born," she said to the woman firmly.

"Oh yes, I will get him to do it. He had to repair it before the last baby."

Shirley wondered what had happened to the door between babies to make it fall off its hinges, but quickly decided that the question was best left unasked!

As she looked around now in the fading light, the sense of responsibility was overwhelming. This was her first baby 'on the district' and as a student midwife she was not supposed to be delivering it alone. A child was asleep in the single bed and the woman herself was on the mattress on the floor. She was groaning loudly. Shirley slipped off her coat and quickly gathered her thoughts together as she called to the husband.

"Right, first of all I need you to move this child somewhere else. Your wife should be the one in the bed, not down there on the floor. Then I will need you to boil a kettle of water and bring it to me. After that, you must get some money into the gas meter before the light goes altogether."

The man looked at Shirley in awe, and silently started his list of chores. He picked up the sleeping child and disappeared from the room. Shirley took this opportunity to examine her patient. She suspected that the woman might be one to make a lot of fuss, but she could not take any chances. She tried to encourage her to move to the bed, but the woman refused and simply groaned louder. The double mattress was pushed up against a wall, and with each groan she shifted closer to the wall and further away from Shirley.

With the light flickering, Shirley knelt on the mattress. To her horror she found that the baby's birth was imminent.

Just then the husband returned. He carried a kettle of water which he handed to Shirley. It was incredibly heavy and Shirley breathed a sigh of relief that she would at least have plenty of hot water.

Her bag was just within reach so she grabbed it and drew out a piece of paper. Turning again towards the husband she spoke urgently.

"My colleague should be with me. Here is her phone number. Be quick now. Go and find a phone box and tell her that I need her urgently. Hurry now. Be quick."

As the man scuttled off down the stairs, Shirley turned back to the woman. Another contraction swept over her and she edged even closer to the wall. Shirley shuffled another few inches to try and keep up with her. It was clear that the baby was going to be born down here on the floor. There was no hope of the woman getting up on the bed at this late stage. As Shirley tended to her, she murmured words of encouragement and reassurance, hoping that they sounded genuine. She dare not consider what could go wrong and her own emotions had to be kept in check. Her back was already aching from being in such an awkward position, and she could feel her legs beginning to go numb from where she was sitting on them.

She quickly pulled a bowl towards her to wash her hands in readiness. She poured in a little cold water from a jug, and then picked up the kettle. But as she started to pour, the water only came out in a trickle and she suddenly realised that it was not full of water at all. It had become furred up and did, in fact, only contain a small amount of water. The rest was hardened deposit.

The woman was caught by another contraction and Shirley could see the baby coming. Her senior midwife was still not there, but she had no choice. She would have to deliver the baby alone. Her back felt as though it was breaking with the effort of leaning over the woman at such a difficult angle.

"OK... now breathe... pant... don't push for a moment..." Shirley urged the woman through the process. "Now, when the next contraction comes, push as hard as you can."

The woman groaned and writhed as the next pain hit her.

At that moment Shirley heard the key in the front door and voices as the midwife and the father started to run up the stairs. At the same moment the woman gave another push and the baby was born. His first cry met them at the bedroom door.

There were a few moments of pandemonium. "What is it?" the mother asked first.

"You have a lovely little boy," Shirley replied, as she felt tears start to prick in her eyes. A birth was always an emotional time and the strain of having been on her own was beginning to catch up with her. Relief washed over her that all was well, and she quickly pushed her own feelings back down.

The father was still trying to catch his own breath and looked a little shaken, but he came closer for a moment and awkwardly touched his son's hand.

The senior midwife was trying to find her own place in the midst of the confusion. The light had just about gone by that stage so she sent the father off with some coins to feed the meter. Shirley handed the screaming, slippery bundle to the senior midwife and then continued to care for the mother. Her legs did not feel as though they belonged to her anymore and she wondered if they would hold her up when she stood, although the 'pins and needles' in them a few moments later quickly told her that circulation was being restored.

The baby was weighed and measured, and the necessary forms completed for the father to take to the Register Office in a few days time. As they sipped a very welcome cup of tea, Shirley and the mother gazed at the new baby. He was wrapped up warm now and had drifted off to sleep.

The mother gently opened the blanket to count his toes. "You know, I have got the others, but a new littl'un is still amazing," she said, and her own tears were now threatening.

"I hope I never get used to the miracle of new birth," Shirley said, as she lifted his tiny hand and held it in her own. She spoke partly to the mother but also to herself. She breathed a silent prayer of thanks to God that all had gone to plan. What would happen to this little boy, she wondered. There was so much poverty. Would he have the opportunity to do something with his life?

When she was satisfied that mother and baby were doing well, Shirley started to pack her things ready to go. She explained to the mother that she would be back the next day. She pulled on her coat and then her eye caught sight of the kettle.

She picked it up and held it high as she smiled at the mother.

"Maybe you should get your husband to buy you a new one of these for Christmas."

Three days later was Christmas morning, and Shirley was once more at the house, doing her daily check on mother and baby. The other children crowded round to watch. Shirley wished them a Happy Christmas and enjoyed a few minutes chatting to them. The mother pointed across the room.

"Look," she said a little shyly. "He did what you said!" And there standing proudly on the table was a brand new tin kettle.

This midwifery experience, although dramatic at the time, gave Shirley a lot of confidence and was to prove invaluable in later years when conditions in which women gave birth were far more primitive.

The years of training had been busy, most of it ward based. It was during her time at *The London* that her attention was drawn to the *Mildmay Mission Hospital* which at that time was a small general hospital in the East End of London. She felt as though she was being guided to do a year of 'staffing' there, although her seniors at *The London* were not altogether happy with the idea.

However, the time at *Mildmay* was priceless. She worked in Out Patients and also in the theatres. As there were no medical students at the hospital, she had opportunities to put in stitches, and generally picked up many valuable techniques. In particular, there was an excellent dentist on the staff who would gladly give lectures to anyone who wanted to listen. Shirley went along to hear his teaching and was then able to practice what she had learnt. After a quick whiff of gas, the dentist pointed to the right instrument, Shirley would give a sharp pull, and if all went well the tooth was out before the patient knew what had happened. If everything did not go quite according to plan, the dentist himself just about had time to do the job before the patient woke up from the anaesthetic!

From *Mildmay* Shirley did a year's training at the *Plaistow Maternity Hospital*, as it was known then. However, during this time a plan was beginning to form in her mind. She decided that she would apply to the London Bible College (LBC) to do a two year Diploma in Theology course once her midwifery studies were complete. She was accepted for training, but there was a six months gap before LBC started, so Shirley and her friend Dorothy had a short time back at *The London* on the maternity wards. They rented a flat together in Clapton. One Christmas they took on some temporary work with the General Post Office (GPO) and found it paid better to deliver parcels instead of babies.

Visits to the family home continued, and Shirley often cycled from central London to Ilford, then on to Chadwell Heath to visit Lil. It was during this time that Shirley came into a deeper relationship with God. She had gradually felt secure in His love, even though at times she felt challenged. But there still seemed to be something missing. She wondered if there was something that she had misunderstood, or whether there was some truth which she had not yet been taught. In talking with her friends at the church, she found that others felt the same. One of them explained that he had come into a new experience which had transformed his relationship with Jesus. Shirley felt excited. She wondered if this was what she was searching for.

Not long after that, an opportunity came to attend a meeting where the ministry of the Holy Spirit was explained, and prayer was offered for those who wanted to be filled with His power. As Shirley responded, she knew that God, through His Spirit, had done another deep work inside her. She felt different.

Her heart ached for Lil to have some sort of hope, and on one of her bike rides home she prayed in tongues – the new language given by the Holy Spirit – that God would give her the opportunity to talk to Lil about spiritual things. She felt Him say, "Ask for a sign".

"What sign shall I ask for?" she prayed, as she negotiated a corner.

She felt God's reply in her heart. "Ask for Lil to initiate a conversation about Me." Having received such a specific answer to her prayer she was encouraged as she continued the long journey. When she reached the hospital she had barely got her coat off and caught her breath, when Lil did just that. Lil had her questions ready and it was not long after that that she came into a relationship with the God of heaven for herself.

Shirley was convinced that Lil would be healed. Her faith was encouraged when Lil began to get some movement in her fingers! That Christmas Lil was allowed home for the first time and Shirley cared for her. The excitement rose! Expectation was high. Back at the hospital, however, Lil suddenly got pneumonia and she was dead within hours. The shock was profound.

In her confusion, Shirley went back to God. "Lord, I thought you were going to heal her." Once again she heard the voice which she had come to recognise. "I have. I've done what you asked."

As the days passed Shirley began to realise that Lil had indeed been healed. She had been fully healed, never to suffer illness and disease again. She realised that Lil was now fully well, and enjoying the presence of God. With that realisation came peace. She also realised that it would have been much more difficult for her to leave England if Lil had still been alive, but that God, in His own gracious and inimitable way, had been working out His perfect plan for them all.

Dorothy and Shirley continued their studies at LBC, cycling from their lodgings in Clapton to the college in Baker Street. One Friday during the second year, Shirley felt pain in her back during the morning cycle ride. She had suffered some back pain before, and as the day progressed it got more and more severe. By the end of lectures she was in so much pain that she could not get onto her bike for the ride home.

In the end they walked back, pushing their bikes as they went. When they got back to the house Dorothy took care of the bikes, bringing them into the hall where they were usually stored, whilst Shirley struggled up the stairs. She was in agony and slowly, painfully, eased herself onto the bed.

The following morning as she tried to get up, the pain was so severe that she passed out and lay in a heap on the floor. Dorothy tried to help her up but it was impossible. Shirley was in too much pain. Dorothy called for an emergency doctor.

"You have a slipped disc," he said, as he prodded and poked. "Stay lying down for two weeks and then come and see me."

"But how do I get her back into bed?" Dorothy was most concerned.

"Don't bother. She can lay there on the floor," he replied, as he headed for the door.

Dorothy enlisted the help of some friends and they removed the mattress from the bed. Then they quite literally rolled Shirley onto it. She was totally helpless.

Sunday was a long and painful day and the night passed slowly. On Monday morning Dorothy left food within Shirley's reach, and then set off for classes. As the door closed, Shirley was overwhelmed with her own utter helplessness. The hours stretched out before her, and there was nothing to do but think, reflect and pray. She wondered if this was a test of her willingness to continue with the calling that God had put on her life. "Yes," she decided. She was still willing, but if she was to complete the task, she needed God to heal her. How could she possibly go to a remote area, travel in canoes and live in the jungle unless her back was up to the task?

If, on the other hand, she had misunderstood God's call and He did not want her to go after all, well, she was willing to accept that decision. It was OK either way.

News of Shirley's condition quickly spread among their friends, and during the day Dorothy bumped into one of the students at college who knew an osteopath working in Harley Street. As soon as she could get away, she cycled to the famous medical road and chained her bike to the railings.

"The doctor does not go out to patients," the receptionist said firmly. "You will have to bring her here." Dorothy was dismayed. How could she possibly get Shirley up off the floor, let alone down the stairs and into a car? She stood silently, wondering what to do.

The consultant's assistant had come out of a room during the conversation and now stood at the desk.

"I will go out and see her," he said gently. "What is the address? I have a cancellation tomorrow. I will go then." His words were spoken with real compassion and Dorothy felt overwhelmed with gratitude. She swallowed hard to deal with the lump in her throat.

Shirley was surprised, but also very relieved when Dorothy returned with news of this development. She had been in so much pain and near to despair. When the osteopath arrived the next day he got down on the floor beside her mattress and did some manipulation on her back. He told her that he had done the best he could in the domestic situation and that she must come to the surgery the following day.

After he had gone, Dorothy quickly got on the phone to see who could come and help them get to Harley Street. She phoned Shirley's father and asked if he could possibly come in his car. Various help was soon volunteered and the next morning some strong chaps heaved Shirley onto a dining room chair and carried her down the three flights of stairs. Her father drove them to Harley Street.

The doctor treated her in the surgery and when she got off the table, it was as though there had never been a problem.

It was now Wednesday, but only the previous Friday she had been told to lay flat on the floor for two weeks. It was amazing! However, the doctor organised some X-rays which showed a defect in the bone. He told Shirley that it could happen again at any time. Life went back to normal but there was niggling doubt and fear. What if it did happen again? What if it happened when she was in a remote jungle area? What if there was no one to help her or manipulate her back? Was she healed or not?

Some time later she was invited to a meeting to share something of her story. The questions over her healing remained but she felt drawn back towards the book of Romans and the life and experiences of Abraham.

Shirley felt convicted in her spirit about her worries and fear, and confessed them to God, surrendering once more to His call on her life and His total ability to see her through. If Abraham had chosen not to consider the weakness of his body, then she would do the same.[5] Once more, she found that surrender brought peace.

Shirley had felt an interest in South America for a long time. During the years of training the interest with that continent began to grow. She had some contact with the Evangelical Union of South America (EUSA) and was anticipating that in due course she would apply to them. Dorothy was interested in the Unevangelised Fields Mission (UFM). They decided that it would be wise not to speak to each other about their feelings until they had each made individual decisions about the future. In this way they could be sure of God's leading, and not be influenced by their friendship.

They had, however, both been to a missionary exhibition where the Wycliffe Bible Translators (WBT) were represented, and had learnt something of their work. After finishing

[5] *And Abraham's faith did not weaken, even though, at about 100 years of age, he figured his body was as good as dead – and so was Sarah's womb. Romans 4:19 New Living Translation (NLT)*

at LBC most people who were expecting to work abroad did a course with Wycliffe, and at that time it was based in Chigwell, not that far from Shirley's home. By now her thoughts had changed completely, and she decided to apply to Wycliffe as a nurse.

During those early introductions to the mission they discovered that it was known as Wycliffe among church groups, but when dealing with universities or official organisations, they used the title 'Summer Institute of Linguistics' (SIL). The Wycliffe course included training to learn a foreign language, particularly if it had never been written down before. Shirley was still expecting to apply as a nurse, but during a lecture, she was really shocked when one of the course leaders challenged her about why she was not going to be a translator.

"Oh, I couldn't do that," she replied quickly.

But even as she said it she knew in her heart that God was challenging her. It did not make sense. She had not enjoyed language study at school and had very negative experiences of language learning there. Neither was she particularly interested. She thought God had called her to be a nurse. Even so, she was convicted that she could not, and should not say "I cannot..." to God.

Shirley knew that she had a gifting towards more analytical approaches, although 'gifting' was probably not the word she would have used at the time. She made a bargain with God. If she got reasonable marks in the exam she would apply as a translator, and if not, she would apply as a nurse. When the results were released the decision was made for her. She had gained adequate results and needed to keep her bargain with God. It now seemed right for her to apply to Wycliffe as a translator, although she felt that all the work she had done to train as a nurse would surely be wasted. To her amazement, Dorothy had also had a change of thinking. She too had been drawn to an interest in Wycliffe, and had also applied to serve with them.

It was September 1960 when Shirley was told that she had been accepted by Wycliffe and would be due to sail at the end of May 1961 – but there were some provisos. It was Wycliffe policy that she would need to find the money for her passage. In addition, she would need to show that she had sufficient financial support for the first three months. It seemed a phenomenal amount and it was not deemed appropriate to ask for money directly.

She realised that she would need to share her vision and calling, not just with friends, but also with people she did not know. She would need to stimulate lots of interest in order to support her future work, both financially and with prayer. But it was not easy to go out to strangers and talk about something which she had not yet done.

It seemed impossible to tackle this challenge whilst doing shift work, and so she decided to leave nursing for the time being and do something which had more regular hours. She applied to the local authority to see if she could do some school work – anything to raise the money she needed. She was accepted immediately, and started work at a school in Barking, close to Ilford.

"Here, Miss, what's your name? Miss, please miss..." It was a little unreal to be standing in a school playground surrounded by five year olds who all wanted their questions answered at once. She was much more familiar with hearing "Nurse! Nurse!" She hoped that the children would learn something along the way, and guessed that she probably would too. Two months into the job she was rather shocked to learn that she was to be given a reception class to teach completely on her own. She had no qualifications but neither did she have time to be scared. This short sharp training session was also to prove invaluable in literacy in days to come.

The weeks sped by and slowly her funds began to gather. To her great excitement she discovered that Dorothy had also been accepted by Wycliffe, and was due to sail at the same time. The days were filled to bursting with necessary paperwork, vaccinations, essential shopping and packing. Before they knew it, May had arrived.

The docks at Southampton were alive with activity. Shirley and Dorothy edged their way through the crowds to meet up with the other ladies who were travelling with them. Her father and Dorothy's parents struggled to keep up. The *SS United States* was a magnificent ship and everyone glanced up at her from time to time in total awe. Her two funnels stood out proudly against the blue sky. She was indeed a luxury liner, and it felt slightly unreal to be waiting to board. She had been dubbed "The fastest liner in the world" and her record was already impressive, having broken that previously set by *HMS Queen Mary*. They had considered what the appropriate dress was in order to travel on such a liner and wore their very best, complete with hats.

When the time came to board, family and friends were allowed to come too, and that helped to ease some of the tension of the occasion. They searched together for the designated cabins and gazed through the porthole windows at the scene below. Vases of flowers were in the cabin and Shirley looked briefly at the cards which accompanied them, knowing that she would have time to think of the senders later. Her emotions were threatening to overwhelm her, but she wanted to keep strong for the sake of her father. She did not know when, or even if, she would see him again. Compassion for him washed over her. This man who had known so much sadness, now had to say "Goodbye" to his only daughter.

The moments passed all too quickly and the signal sounded for friends and family to say their final farewells and to leave the ship. She could feel him trembling as she gave him a final hug and then watched his every move as he worked his way down the gangway.

The people on the quayside looked so small, and she lost sight of him from time to time, but managed to pick him out again and they waved to each other once more. There was plenty of activity as the crew completed their final preparations. The engines were throbbing now, and the ship gave a blast from the funnels which made them all jump.

The passengers clung to the handrails, each one now desperately wanting a last look at their family and friends. Shirley and her father had another wave as the huge vessel slowly began to move.

SS United States

3 June bugs

When the people on the shore were too small to recognise, Shirley and her friends made their way back to their cabins. They were all emotionally exhausted. By now the porters had delivered their luggage, and it was good to have something to do as they started to unpack and look around. An information folder, adorned with the ship's crest, contained instructions on how to find the dining room. Details on mealtimes, safety measures and routines on board were also given. They changed their clothes and generally freshened up, then headed out to wander around on deck before searching out the dining room.

Dinner was a sumptuous affair. They felt like royalty and were a bit uncomfortable at being waited on hand and foot. They were all more at ease in serving others. However, they decided to make the most of this time of luxury and settled down to enjoy each course.

The crew were obviously proud of their vessel and at various times during the voyage would give talks about her. They learned that the ship had been specifically designed to be as fireproof as possible and, as a result, the only ordinary piece of wood on board was the butcher's block in the galley. All other furniture and fittings were custom-made in glass, metal and spun glass fibre to meet the stringent fire regulations.

Each meal proved to be a grand affair. It was like having Christmas dinner three times a day. Shirley, however, had always suffered with travel sickness, and she struggled now with the rich food, and the gentle but constant movement of the ship. Sometimes she just longed for something simple like a piece of bread and butter.

Although it was now June, the weather was cool and it was chilly to sit on deck. Even so, it was a good place to rest and reflect on all that had been happening in the last months and years.

The journey across the Atlantic took no more than four or five days, and it was not long before anticipation mounted among the passengers for glimpses of America. The closer they got, the warmer it became. Inspirational talks now moved from the ship to the Statue of Liberty, which would be one of their first sights of America.

They knew that it was a symbol of freedom and democracy which was known around the world, but now learned that it had been a present from the people of France in 1886 in recognition of the friendship established between them during the American Revolution.

"It is more than just a monument," one patriotic American passenger declared. "It is a beloved friend, a living symbol of freedom to millions around the world."

Excitement mounted as they approached America and the statue was certainly an inspiring sight against the equally magnificent skyline of New York. Although the voyage had been a privilege and a most interesting experience, Shirley was not sorry to leave the ship and to step once more onto solid ground.

New York was hot; very hot. The customs hall was a-buzz of hustle and bustle with crowds of people jostling to get through, and each one wanting to be on their way. Shirley had tied her luggage with some new – and rather expensive – cord which she planned to use at jungle camp. She was horrified when one of the customs officers cut it all off, but then gave no more than the briefest look inside. They were all still on emotional overload and moments such as these seemed overwhelming. Sea sickness, heat, culture and time changes were all catching up with her, to say nothing of the huge emotion of leaving the familiar territory of England for somewhere totally unknown. Shirley explained to the officer that they had much further to travel and asked him to re-tie the luggage for her. He did, although he used much thinner cord. He used a metal strap on her case and tied it so tightly that it was cutting into the leather.

They were all dog-tired and only longed for something simple to eat and the chance to sleep in a proper bed. Their hosts, however, were full of enthusiasm to talk, and plan the sightseeing itineraries for the next couple of days. However, by the next morning they were somewhat revived and ready to set out and catch a proper glimpse of New York.

First impressions of America were dominated by the size of everything. Houses, shops, cars... everything was massive! The next surprise was that most meals were taken out, even breakfast. The price of food seemed on the high side and they were cautious of spending too much. The cost of the official tours around the city seemed to be exorbitantly high, so they were more than happy for their hosts to give them an unofficial tour. It was certainly an experience to go up the Empire State Building and they were so relieved that there was a lift! A quarter of a mile off the ground, the Observatory gave them a stunning view down to Fifth Avenue and across the rooftops and avenues of the New York Metropolitan area. At the top it was pointed out to them that four states could be seen. They took some photos from the 86th floor where the cars on the streets below looked just like toys. They also saw the United Nations Building and then, in the evening, set out on a long walk to see the lights of the city at night.

On the following day they did some shopping for the next stage of their journey, but needed to get a reasonably early night ready to catch the Greyhound Bus at 3.40am the following morning. Their hosts arranged for a taxi to take them to the bus station. The lady driver arrived in a very large car but they quickly filled it with their luggage. She seemed a rather coarse sort of woman, but before long they were very grateful for her no-nonsense approach as she negotiated them through the process of having their luggage checked.

The coach seemed comfortable and as they settled in they tried out the various buttons. The seats reclined and that was a relief. There was air conditioning too. Since they were not due in the Oklahoma area until 10.30pm the following day, it was reassuring to know that there would be some comfort during the 44 hours or so onboard.

For the first few hours they were happy just to sit and take in the scenery. Tunnels took them through the mountains, and the countryside was breathtakingly beautiful. Shirley was fascinated by the bridge systems and intersections, and marvelled at the quality – and size – of the roads. The coach made good speed and they overtook many cars. The day dragged on slowly. They ate some of their food, dozed a bit, chatted for a while, and at other times gazed out of the windows, each lost in their own thoughts. At one point they passed a herd of buffalo, and a little further along the road were amused to see a restaurant which was advertising buffalo burgers.

At some point during that first night the coach pulled into a bus station. It was a relief to get out and stretch their legs. They walked around for a few minutes, and then sat down to have a bite to eat. Just then, they felt as though they were being attacked. Great big beetles seemed to appear from nowhere, hit the lights and then dived towards them. They were all taken by surprise and quite terrified. They leapt up and ran to another seat but it seemed as though the bugs were everywhere. They were simply enormous.

As the driver returned from his break they gathered around him to ask about the bugs.

"Oh yes. June bugs. That's what they are known as round here. They are harmless enough. They are attracted by the light. You'll get used to them," he said nonchalantly as he climbed back into his seat. "All aboard now, we are about to leave."

As Shirley settled back into her seat her emotions threatened once more. She had not been mentally prepared for insects and creepy crawlies quite so soon. Her own reaction had shaken her. She realised just how frightened she had been. As the bus pulled out and back onto the highway, she gazed silently out of the window into the darkness. She realised that this was an important moment. The Lord had made these creatures. She was going to meet many of them during her life's work. She had a choice about how she would respond in the future. In that moment, she decided that she would choose not to be scared and more than that, even to like them.

The bus made an unscheduled stop at some point as the driver was having trouble with the brakes. In the end they had to change buses, and the delay meant that it was much later than expected when they finally arrived exhausted at their destination. For a moment they wondered why the driver had not gone right in, but then realised that the bus station was closed. They gathered around the luggage area to wait for their bags. None appeared. Their luggage was not on this bus as it had not been transferred at the change over. To add to their misery, the pavement was simply covered with June bugs. The resolve which Shirley had made earlier in the bus was now severely tested.

They gazed around, bewildered. They were grateful that they did at least have the address of the place where they were to stay, and someone found them a taxi. They climbed in and sped off into the darkness. It was a huge relief that a few people were still up at the centre when they arrived. Within a few minutes an assorted collection of pyjamas appeared, they were given a drink and guided to a mattress. A curtain would suffice as a sheet. They were past caring. They lay down and slept.

With the beginning of a new day they could take stock of where they were. The linguistics course run by Wycliffe's Summer Institute of Linguistics, was held on the campus of the university in the town of Norman, just outside Oklahoma City. The centre was a series of red brick buildings set amid lawns and mature trees. Dorothy and Shirley found themselves sharing a room once more. Just outside their window two pine trees gave some welcome shade from the scorching sun and also provided a good place for bird watching. On the door of their room a scroll declared, "Hitherto hath the Lord helped us". How true that must have been for the many people who had passed through this centre over the years, and it was good to be reminded once more of the faithfulness of God.

It was extremely hot although the occasional, but rather violent thunderstorms did bring some welcome relief. Cold showers were also a luxury! Their luggage finally arrived which was also a great relief. Before them was another period of study and in the oppressive heat, it was hard to settle. From time to time memories of home washed over Shirley and caught her by surprise. A letter from her father told her of some puppies which had been born to their dog Susie, and she could visualise him trying to hold all four of them at once. As she pictured the scene, England suddenly seemed very far away.

One Sunday evening after church they were all invited to the home of a doctor. His house was fabulous and they were made very welcome. The ice-cream, coffee and cookies on the veranda made a welcome break. As darkness fell around 8pm the insects started to gather, and so they made their way inside the house to enjoy a singsong around the piano.

Shirley began to write to her father on a weekly basis, and he responded with many questions. She tried to explain the different courses to him:

"My dear dad,

I did receive your first letter OK. Thanks. There are several courses running simultaneously here. The First Year is the same as the course we did at Chigwell last year, so we are not required to do that. The Intermediate is mainly revision of the First Year, and some practical work with speakers of the local ethnic languages. The emphasis of this course is on language learning. The Second Year includes some revision from the previous year, and a lot of reading about the different approaches and methods of analysis used by all the main linguists over the past thirty years. The Third Year is the more advanced study with particular emphasis on solving the problems of the language which I, and others 'in the field', will be working on. We can choose which course we want to do. Dorothy is doing the Intermediate course, and I have chosen the Second Year. We can either study in our rooms or in the library. We tend to do most of it in the library so that we have access to the many books which we need."

Each day they spent an hour of conversational practice with one of the language helpers who came into the centre. Around the State of Oklahoma there were various ethnic groups speaking their own language, and some of these were willing to help teach Cheyenne or Kiowa. These language helpers introduced Shirley and her friends to some of the beautiful bead work and other traditional crafts from their people groups. On the way back from church one day they had the opportunity to stop at a museum, and were fascinated with what they saw. Intricate headdresses made from beautifully coloured feathers, together with shoes and coats in the most complex patterns were breathtaking to see. The museum also had models of different activities, including riding, hunting and traditional weapons.

The days seemed to be hectic and were getting hotter, with the temperature rising to the upper 90s (about 35°C). It seemed as though study stretched out before Shirley with no end in sight. She had already done so much work to train as a nurse and midwife, as well as completing time at Bible College back in England. Was that all wasted, she wondered? Now before her was a seemingly endless list of things to complete on translation and linguistics, both written and practical. Sometimes it felt as though she was like a clock, going round and round, hour after hour, day after day and week after week. She wondered if she would ever make it to the actual work which she felt God had called her to do. When that day did come, she would have to start studying all over again. She knew that each ethnic group had their own spoken language, with nothing written down. At that stage the challenge of translation would be ever harder, and it was a sobering thought. Language study still did not come easily and it required so much discipline.

It was good to snatch moments of rest and relaxation from time to time. Unlike most of the country, the students did not get time off for Independence Day. One evening they were able to pile into a friend's car with a picnic and have a change of scene from the campus. A turtle ambling across the road caused an impromptu stop, and while they waited for it to complete its crossing, discovered a flattened snake which had not been so successful. They took a welcome swim, and then shared their picnic with various bugs and insects.

Lectures often went on into the evening and it was frequently quite late before the students could take a walk to enjoy the grounds in the cooler air. It was fun to identify some of the groups of stars shining out of a clear night sky. Many luminous bugs were around in the evenings and the noise they made was incredible.

Shirley was encouraged one evening to discover that she could understand more than she thought she would, although she could not tell whether that was the result of her improvement or if the lectures were getting simpler. She recounted to her father that it was only the intelligent ones who ventured to ask a question, while the rest of them tried to look as though they knew exactly what was being said.

Violent storms seemed to be the norm and Shirley would sometimes lie awake at night as the lightning flashed through the room every couple of seconds, illuminating the whole sky. The thunder was reminiscent of air raids and sent a shiver down her spine. One building was hit during their time on campus but no significant damage was done. The rain was often torrential. A tornado warning system was in place at the campus.

The rain cleared one evening in time for a surprise picnic for Shirley's birthday. Some of the other girls had been out and bought steaks, which they cooked over a charcoal fire. They only had one knife between the seven of them, and a single plastic fork. The same picnic site also had a games area with free equipment which could be used by all and sundry. A game of shuffleboard rounded off the evening nicely.

The days were packed with activity and it was hard to keep the right balance on priorities as work piled up. Shirley found that her tape recorder was a mixed blessing as the reel to reel machine could not always take different size spools. The one which she owned personally took small reels, and those could also be played on a tape recorder designed for larger sizes. If, however, she received a large spool, her machine would not accommodate it and she was not able to listen.

The typewriter too, was often unpredictable. She had a project to complete on the subject of Machine Translation - in anticipation of the days when they might be able to use computers - and the deadline was fast approaching when it had to be submitted. After typing for five hours one day her arms felt as though they were about to drop off.

Cameras and film were another issue. Films were sent by post to *Ilford Ltd* in England for processing, and were then returned to her the same way. The potential for precious photos to be lost en route was considerable. With all the packing and unpacking which had to be done, the various pieces of equipment took a fair amount of knocks along the way, none of which did them any good. The humidity also took a toll on all kinds of machines.

Exams were looming. They needed to get visa extensions, and all this took time. The course was coming to an end and there was packing to do as well. They had found that kit bags were not altogether satisfactory, as porters tended to drag them along the ground, which quickly made holes in the material. Even before they had left England, the advice had been to use drums which had previously been used for dry products. These had lids on top and could be sealed and secured with a padlock. Because they had all accumulated extra things along the way they needed to acquire another drum before they moved on again.

Letters between Shirley and her father continued regularly, both of them writing to each other most weeks. At one point Shirley found that she had 55 letters from various other people awaiting a response. The thought that so many people were interested in her work and cared about her, was both humbling and comforting, but it was hard at times to keep up with the responses which she wanted to give. It all took time. She did not miss the television much but would have liked a bit more world news. She considered buying a short wave radio but decided against it. It would be one more thing to carry, and was unlikely to survive the intense humidity. Just once in a while though, she longed to hear the familiar tones of Big Ben. Snippets of national and international news came through her father's letters, and if she remembered, she would ask him for an update. By the time she got the response, however, the event was often long gone.

The intense, three month course at Norman, Oklahoma, was coming to an end, and packing was completed in earnest.

Next stop was Sulphur Springs, Arkansas, for a conference. It only took place once every two years and was a big affair. It was a welcome break from study, at least for a while. It was relief to see hills and valleys, creeks and streams again after the rather flat area of Norman and the atmosphere of a campus. Shirley's group of friends were amongst the first to arrive at Sulphur Springs. 250 people were expected, with some of them coming from around the world.

There were several big houses set in lovely surroundings, and every inch of space was going to be needed for the event. The group were shown to their accommodation which was a dormitory sleeping about 60 people. This was going to be another new experience. There was hardly time to stack away their luggage before they were called to help clean some of the other rooms ready for guests, and were even asked to do some painting to freshen up a few rather scruffy areas. Last minute preparations were frantic.

As soon as they had completed the allotted tasks, they were asked to help prepare vegetables for the first meal. Guests were arriving all the time and Shirley was rather startled to see one family come with mother, father, children, one brightly coloured parrot, a small monkey and a baby ocelot – which thankfully was on a lead! It was much later before they had the chance to take a stroll in the grounds. They wandered down towards the river and it was not long before the pungent smell of sulphur hit them. It was clear how Sulphur Springs got its name. There were three springs at the bottom of the hill, and Shirley dipped a finger into one of the springs and cautiously tasted the water. It reminded her of indigestion mixture. She decided not to taste the other two, the smell of rotten eggs being more than enough to discourage the idea.

As the conference got under way the sessions proved to be encouraging and uplifting.

Reports of projects and amazing answers to prayer could not fail to increase their faith and expectancy. It was reported that all the different ethnic groups in Ecuador now had translators working in them. On the other side of the picture, they were also reminded of the huge number of people groups which were still un-reached, and her sense of calling was once more renewed. It was strange at first to see some of the women take sewing or other craft projects into the meetings with them, although it was clearly an accepted practice, but in time Shirley herself found that it was more relaxing to listen to the various speakers when her own fingers were busy.

There was great anticipation over the expected visit of Rachel Saint, the sister of Nate, one of the five missionaries who had been killed by the Auca* Indians in Ecuador just a few years previously. Their martyrdom had shocked the whole world. Rachel brought with her a lady called Dayuma, one of the Auca ladies who had escaped from her village. Shirley met her briefly in the kitchen, but the language barrier prevented any meaningful conversation.

A visit to the missionary 'barrel' proved worthwhile. Various people sent in clothes, and a dry cleaning company donated items which had not been collected. There were vast amounts of clothing, some of which seemed almost new. Shirley was delighted to gain a new dress, and also a couple of shirts which would be useful at jungle camp. She could have taken more, but once again, the thought of handling all her luggage was always in her mind.

The conference ended and farewells were said to old and new friends. They planned to spend the weekend in Dallas before heading off to the border into Mexico. The hospitality there was given by two separate families, so they spent much of the day with one family, and slept at the home of the other.

* *The Auca people call themselves Waorani*

They were made so welcome and once again, gave thanks for God's people along the way. Both houses were beautiful and in the one where they slept, they shared their room with the stuffed head of a goat, three deer and a moose! All these had been caught personally by their host. The gadgets in the house were a real novelty, especially a dishwasher. They were fascinated too by the car with automatic gears and electric windows. This was, after all, the early 1960s.

The weekend passed all too quickly and it was soon time to board a bus which would take them to the Mexican border. They were grateful to have the company of some Wycliffe members who were experienced in this part of the journey. At the border town of Laredo they discovered that some of their metal drums had been taken to another bus station. A taxi was sent to collect them – at the expense of the bus company – and the bus driver waited, more or less patiently, for the luggage to be reunited with its owners. The next hurdle was Customs, where every bag, box and drum had to be opened. Shirley had secured the drums tightly by hand, but even with a crowbar, the customs officer had to try for some while to get them open. There followed a brief examination of the contents before they were closed up again. It was a great relief that all seemed to be in order, and no charges were made.

Back on the bus, and twenty miles along the road, they were stopped at a checkpoint. It was then discovered that their papers had not been stamped correctly. Although they could have been sent back to the border, it was a relief to be dealt with kindly, and after having thumb prints taken, they were on their way once more. The rest of the 1000 mile journey, although long and very tiring, was uneventful and the scenery was a constant source of wonder with mountains, deserts and huge cactus plants of all shapes and sizes.

Once more it was a relief to get off the bus in Mexico City, although the noise which hit them was hard to describe. Cars screeched in and out, driving at breakneck speed and barely slowing down for the corners. Shirley watched in amazement. Very few vehicles seemed to have silencers and to add to the mayhem, large rattling trams clattered down the centre of the roads.

One afternoon Shirley and Dorothy took a long walk out to a famous castle and visited a circular museum which housed a fascinating history of the whole country. They came back in a 'one peso' taxi and so added public transport in Mexico City to their fast growing list of experiences. They had shared so much up to this point, both back in England and also on the journey so far, but now their paths were to separate for a while. Shirley was advised that she and two other ladies were on assignment to a Chinanteco village for the next six weeks. There had been a work in progress for about eight years, but ill health among the missionary workers had brought it to a halt.

The journey to the Chinanteco village took two days, and they stopped overnight at a beautiful hotel. Not quite so idyllic was the paratyphoid which Shirley picked up while she was there. Fortunately she was able to get antibiotics from a local doctor once they had arrived at the Chinanteco community.

During their stay in the village the next door neighbour's dog seemed to adopt them. One Sunday they set out for church and noticed that the dog was coming too. He came into the church with them and quietly sat under their bench. The service was being conducted in Spanish, and Shirley did not understand a word. She was rather shocked when one of her colleagues nudged her and said that it had just been announced that the three visiting ladies would be singing to them. Before she knew what was happening they were at the front, hastily deciding what to sing. 'The Lord's my Shepherd' seemed a safe enough choice. To their horror though, the person leading the music started on a tune which was totally unknown to them. At that moment the dog came out from under the bench and went forward, to sit in front of them like a conductor. It was almost impossible to keep a straight face.

4 Jungle camp

There were plenty of horror stories about jungle camp. The three month's training in southern Mexico was divided into two sections. The first six weeks were spent at 'main base' which was set in a beautiful location beside the mountains in the valley known as Yaxoquintela – the Valley of the Running Green Water. Lessons were mainly on survival in the jungle with practical teaching in canoeing, swimming, hiking, farming and first aid.

The girls' dormitory was a long thatched hut which had mud walls, and was divided into four separate rooms. Dorothy and Shirley shared one of these rooms. It had very basic furniture, some of which looked as though it was the result of experiments from former students in carpentry classes. One chair was clearly not fit for the purpose and would never have received 'Health and Safety' approval!

The first and rather important lesson was how to get into a jungle hammock. This had a waterproof base and a triangular-shaped waterproof roof. Between the two there was netting. In theory, you climbed up into the hammock and zipped yourself in, safe from insects. In practice, it was a tricky manoeuvre. The hammock had a tendency to start swinging once the person had got into it, and if you were not careful it would turn over completely. At that stage the occupant could easily become trapped and it was very difficult to get out, unless there was someone on the outside to lend a hand. It took quite a bit of practice to master the knack of getting in gently, and then keeping still until the rocking had stopped. Only then could they cautiously adjust their position to do up the long zip. There were some hilarious moments until they had all managed to perfect the technique. Once in, however, and zipped up tight, it was reasonably comfortable, unless of course the occupant needed to go out in the dark to make a visit.

On the second day there were instructions in how to saddle, mount and ride a mule and this also provided a great deal of hilarity. In time, however, it seemed that walking was by far the easiest option. The mules – noted for their obstinacy – proved true to character, and preferred to walk on the edge of the road where it was slightly less muddy. That meant the rider was dragged through the thistles and brambles. If they did not have their wits about them, they could easily lose a hat in the bushes and be in danger of losing their head or a leg in the same way. Shirley's mule had a mind of its own and chose to jump the narrow ditches and tree trunks which were lying in the path, which sent her flying up in the air and landing painfully on the wooden saddle.

There were daily swimming lessons in a nearby river. Shirley could already swim well, having gained a life saving certificate at school. Her favoured strokes were breaststroke and backstroke. They were encouraged to try new ones, but it was quite a challenge to do the crawl against the strong currents. Some of the group could not swim at all, and close attention was given to help them along. It was already clear that falling in the fast flowing water would be an occupational hazard, and being able to swim could make the difference between life and death.

For three weeks the girls had carpentry lessons while the men did mechanics. They were taught a little about basic tools, but the main challenge was to make a piece of furniture out of tree branches. They had to be able to demonstrate that the item could serve the purpose for which it had been built. After much banging, hammering and sawing in the carpentry room, their bedroom had the addition of a table and a shoe-rack.

After three weeks the men and the ladies changed groups. The study of mechanics was fairly basic with teaching on different types of pressure lamps and blow torches, and then some instruction on how to solder things together. The art of sharpening knives was also really important. The lectures on outboard motors began to get a bit lost on the female minds, and they realised that if one went wrong they would be unlikely to have the tools or the knowledge to fix it without some outside help.

The days were filled to capacity and the outdoor life gave them a hearty appetite. Each group either had to prepare one meal of the day or wash up after one meal, both of which took an extraordinary amount of time. The breakfast crew had to be up at 4am in order to get the fire going and have breakfast prepared by 6.15am. Although they were as careful as they could be to avoid food contamination, Shirley often wondered about the mouthfuls of water which she swallowed during swimming lessons.

Each of them had to learn how to kill a chicken, and that proved to be quite a challenge for some. The gift of a cow was very welcome and there was some discussion on the best way to slaughter it. The general consensus was that a well aimed shot would be the best method. It was a mammoth task to skin the animal and as many people as possible were called in to help. By late afternoon they had still not finished, so some of the group got up at 4am the next morning to complete the job of boning and cutting up the meat. Some was minced and other cuts put into preserving jars. The food, although unconventional at times, was good and plentiful, which was all that they were really concerned about. Bread and butter had, by now, disappeared from their diet but there were plenty of other new things to try. They were so hungry that they would have eaten almost anything.

Christmas came during their time at main base and with it, the weather turned chilly and wet. The 'postman' – a pilot from the Missionary Aviation Fellowship (MAF) - brought a few welcome letters and cards. They made each other a few

Christmas presents in the carpentry shop and had many laughs over the back scratcher which one of the chaps had made from a chicken's leg tied to a stick.

One whole day was spent baking and they experimented with different kinds of bread, sweet bread and cinnamon rolls. They decorated the latter with icing and nuts. It was Shirley's turn to kill a chicken, something most of them had done about three times already, so they were beginning to understand the anatomy of their feathered friends. She and Dorothy made a tasty Christmas pudding and even managed to rustle up custard to go with it.

The seven girls were all late for breakfast on Christmas morning as they had been having so much fun in the girls' dorm, but they made such a noise on their entrance, banging buckets and tin bowls, and singing modified words to the tune of 'Jingle Bells', that it seemed as though no one noticed that they were late. There were one or two families with children among the group so there was a good excuse for everyone to throw themselves into the Christmas spirit.

With Christmas celebrations over, life quickly returned to whatever was classed as normal in main base. Each day brought lectures on customs and cultures. They were also sent out in small groups to the scattered houses in the locality. They would be given some phrases to elicit, and by acting out 'carrying wood' or 'making a chair' they were expected to come back with the appropriate phrase.

During the time at main base, they made some visits into surrounding villages inhabited by members of the Tzeltal people. During the previous ten years more than 6000 of these people had come to faith in God, and it was so good to sit and worship with them in their young church. They also visited the Lacandon people but the comparison was startling. Although the two ethnic groups were comparatively near to each other geographically, in spiritual understanding they were poles apart, the Lacandon having resisted the gospel for 16 years. They still made clay god pots which were the focal point of their worship. Even though it was so sad that these people had rejected the truth, the contrast, nevertheless, made a deep impression on Shirley and strengthened her resolve and calling to bring the good news of Jesus Christ to people who had never had the chance to hear it for themselves.

The time at main base was nearing its completion, and their thoughts turned more and more to the next stage of the training. There was so much to do in preparation. The journey to 'advance base' started with a rise from bed at 3am and they were ready to hit the trail at 6am for the 20 mile walk. There were a few mules for the children, the luggage and slower walkers. The rest of the group were allowed to ride for one hour in every three or four. It was a long, hot day.

They arrived at the location by around mid afternoon and sat down wearily to await further instructions. The mules too, seemed more than ready for a break. But the rest did not last for long. Instructions were then given that the group would be divided into twos. Each pair would be sent off into virgin jungle without knowing where anyone else was. They were to set up their own base camp, and use machetes to build a *champa* – a small wooden shack – and organise themselves to live there for the next six weeks. They were told that they would be called together at various times for group activities, but their base camp would be just for the two of them. They were given a quantity of left-over food to heat up that night, and were reminded to make sure it was completely hot.

It had been a long, hard day. They gathered round the pile of luggage to retrieve their own packs, and hoisted them up onto their backs. They were now very short of water, the packs were extremely heavy and before them the jungle vines stood some 20 – 40 feet high. This was not quite the same as the adventure at main base. It was altogether more serious.

Dorothy and Shirley had been paired off together and it was such a relief to be setting out with someone who was already a good friend. Around their waist they each had a survival kit which contained essential items such as water purification tablets, salt tablets, matches and so on. They both also carried a tin water bottle which held about two pints of water. It was in a double casing so that the outer section could be used for cooking. This was also carried from the waist but, by now, was almost empty.

They had become quite proficient at using a machete, and had been told that they should have one with them at all times. Once having been given instructions on the direction they were to travel, they set to, cutting down the vines and hacking their way through the deep jungle growth. They found what looked like a suitable location and dropped their packs in order to catch their breath and look around.

They needed to get a fire going as soon as possible and certainly before night closed in. On the other hand, they needed to get some sort of shelter built, and to get their hammocks organised for the night. Having mastered the art of getting into a jungle hammock at main base, they decided to get those up first, so that at least one job would be done. These were swung from the trees fairly quickly. The *champa* would have to wait.

Lighting the fire was not so easy. The jungle wood was very damp so it was a struggle. Light was fading and the ladies realised that they were running out of time. They placed their pan of food over the flickering flame and stirred it hopefully, tasting it now and again. It was barely warm. Hunger was now getting the better of them and they took a few more spoonfuls.

There seemed to be so many insects around – more than they had ever known before – and these added to their discomfort. They wondered if they were attracted by the smoke or the fire. Just then, realisation dawned. They were about to be invaded by army ants. Both of them jumped up instinctively and headed for their individual hammocks. They knew it was a race against time. The ants were already swarming over the food in the pan and were marching towards the trees which held their hammocks. They were an awesome and terrifying sight. Shirley struggled with the netting and heaved herself in while the hammock rocked perilously. She dare not wait until the rocking had stopped and quickly zipped it up, hoping that she was in time, and that it would not flip over. The idea of aggressive army ants inside her hammock was frightening. She hardly dared to breathe as she lay there in the darkness, terrified that the ants would find a way in somewhere. Darkness had come quickly and the thick canopy of the trees overhead blotted out any glimpse of the sky. Even a few twinkling stars would have been some company. She called across to Dorothy and was relieved to know that she was also in her hammock.

It was hard to know how much time had passed but it felt like several hours. It was now pitch dark. Shirley began to feel nausea rising in her stomach. She knew that the food had not been re-heated sufficiently, and although they had not eaten a full meal, it was enough. She was scared that she would start to vomit. As she lay there feeling wretched, she realised that the effects of the food were working their way through her system and that before long, she would simply have to get out of the hammock and find somewhere discreet. Was it safe now from the ants? There was only one way to find out.

It was a huge relief when dawn broke the following morning and they could see what they were doing once again. Both of them felt exhausted and rather fragile, but daylight gave them the opportunity to get themselves a little more organised. It was important to get the *champa* built as soon as possible, but even more pressing was the need for water.

They could hear a river nearby and followed the sound of it, stepping carefully across the jungle floor, hacking a way through as they went. There were trees of varying sizes with the occasional tree trunk blocking their way.

It was so good to step out into a clearing and to see blue sky once more. They were desperately thirsty and it was a huge relief to collect some water and to have a swim to freshen up. They also needed to wash some clothes. Those from the previous day were absolutely filthy. They had brought three sets each: one to wear, one to wash and the other drying out. It had been surprising to find just how long clothes did take to dry in the humid conditions, even though it was so hot, and they never really felt, or smelt, particularly clean. Once back at their camp site, they hung the clothes out to dry over the branches of some trees. The next most important task was to sort out their food supplies, and to get them as far off the ground as possible.

They sat for a short while to consider the best building plan. By now they both felt very weary but realised the importance of having a shelter as soon as possible. As they sat there, they encouraged the fire to burn, feeding it gently with twigs. It was good to see the smoke lazing skyward, and to feel the sense of accomplishment that they had won a further battle with the elements. Once the fire was blazing well, they were able to cook some food, and enjoyed their first real meal out there alone in the jungle. It tasted wonderful and they could both feel strength returning with every mouthful.

With renewed vigour they picked up their machetes and started to cut down some branches. It was a slow process and they needed to modify their original plan, but slowly and surely a little shack began to take shape. Later that day they celebrated with another meal under its canopy, and were more than ready when darkness fell and it was time to climb into their hammocks, slightly more gently than the night before. As they woke sleepily the next morning they decided to name their new home 'Paradise Lost and Almost Regained'!

Each pair of recruits was given the same basic kind and amount of provisions. It included rice, macaroni, flour, oil, sugar and salt, and these had to last them the whole six weeks. If they used them too quickly, it would be a hard lesson to learn, but it was part of the training to teach them to make adequate shopping lists.

They did get some fresh food from a group of Tzeltal who used to come by with eggs, fruit and occasionally a chicken or other meat. The person who was in charge of the advance camp would use any available money to pay them, and supplies were shared so that everyone received the same amount of food.

After a few days they all discovered that they could make some sort of bush telegraph system. By shouting at the top of their voices they could send a message to their nearest neighbours, who in turn sent it on to the next group. It led to some interesting mix ups. This system was used, from time to time, to bring the whole group together.

Those moments were really great. Some had horror stories to add to the anecdotes about advance base, while others had successes to recount. It was certainly good just to see other humans again. Shirley and Dorothy recounted their rather dramatic story of the army ants but no one else seemed to have had a similar problem.

The times together usually involved more teaching. One important lesson on a hike into the jungle was to learn about the types of vine which held water in their stem. Other lessons included swimming and first aid. One afternoon they had a 'pot luck' supper on the beach, using chayotes instead of potatoes. These were prickly, green, pear-shaped vegetables. They boiled them in their skins and then cut off the outside, before frying the inner part, which tasted surprisingly like chips.

During the time at advance base, each group was expected to do an overnight canoe trip which should include at least two bends in the river. They could decide themselves whether to go up or downriver. Dorothy and Shirley decided to go upriver, although it was a real battle against the current which turned them round and round several times. Realising that they were going nowhere, in the end they swam, pushing the canoe as they went. It was quite a relief to reach a spot where they could make camp. By now they had become experts at making a fire, and it did not take long to get one going, with supper then ready within ten minutes.

The return trip the next morning was done by torch light. They were slightly taken aback by two beady eyes which reflected from the water in the light of the torch, and were relieved to find them belonging to nothing more dangerous than a rather large toad.

One morning the group was brought together and informed that they were going on a survival hike. They had just 30 minutes to prepare a small pack of basic supplies which would be brought to them later. There was no time for dinner, and they set off around midday with their survival kit, machete, a canteen of water and a hat.

A canoe with an outboard motor took them upstream for about half an hour, where they were put ashore with two of the staff. They were told to make a jungle clearing of at least 25 paces apart - and out of sight of each other - and then set up home for the night. They should get what food and firewood that they could. They were told to build a 'lean-to' and to make a bed on which to sleep. They did not have hammocks, mosquito nets or anything else at all. They had to construct something from what they could find.

They found plenty of jungle celery which they tried to cook with a salt tablet from the survival kit, but it was hard to get down and was actually easier to eat raw. Once it was dark, a staff member came round secretly to check on them from time to time. Shirley was surprised how well she slept. Perhaps it was from sheer exhaustion.

The following morning she went down to the river and looked longingly at the large fish which were swimming close to the edge. However, there was nothing with which to catch them and so they lived to swim another day. Around 9am they heard the *chug chug* of the motor boat in the distance and each received a welcome bar of chocolate, together with the packs which they had prepared the day before.

The test was by no means over. At 10.30am the group was divided into two – the 'lost' and the 'found'. The lost group were taken upriver and put off on a beach. They had to start finding their own way back to base. The rest of the party were told to set out to find them. They had until 1pm the following day. If they had not succeeded by that time, they were to return to base and enlist more help.

Shirley was part of the found group and they were allowed to take as much water as they could carry. They were told not to go back to the river, but for the rest of the day they were to pretend that they could not find any more when the water ran out. The lesson on jungle vines now proved invaluable, but they were all still parched. The few drops of water from the vines barely seemed to wet their mouths. They were led into the jungle and told to set up base camp for the night. It took six of them three hours to get the large construction finished.

That night they were all exhausted. They were hungry and thirsty too. They had been told to make a fire and to keep it going all night as protection from any animals which might be nearby, but it was a real temptation just to lie down on their make-shift bed and fall asleep. However, they did manage to keep the fire going between them on a rota system, but they still woke with a start when a jungle tapir came striding through the camp at some unearthly hour.

The next day the searchers set off through the jungle to try and find the lost group. They marked their journey with trails so that they would not get lost themselves. It was a triumphant moment when they all found each other and arrived back at the base together.

Towards the end of the experience at advance base, they were all taken to a remote area. They had started out with their usual can of water each and had been able to replenish them when they stopped at a very beautiful location for a lunch break. However, they got so thirsty in the hot and humid conditions and there never seemed to be enough water available. When they came to their destination they were told that they were to make camp for the night. They found out later that the place had a name which meant 'Hidden Water'.

As they looked around to get their bearings they saw a large puddle. Hanging over it was a bamboo pipe which had been previously erected. It had been cut lengthways rather like a gutter, and was obviously meant to channel water down from the surrounding hill. At the centre of the puddle and underneath the bamboo device, was a large stone. It appeared that by standing on the stone, the water cans could be refilled from the supply from above. The problem was that the water was only coming slowly... drip... drip... drip.

Some of the group decided to climb the hill and investigate the source of the water. To their horror they found that there was another puddle at the top around which various animals were obviously contaminating the water with their faeces. This was the water which they were collecting below.

It was, however, the only water source available, and so in desperation they collected what they could, boiled it vigorously, added water purification tablets and hoped for the best. It still tasted foul. As they reflected later in the day they realised that it was so easy to read the scriptures and think of people like the Children of Israel[6] who quickly started to grumble when things went wrong. It was easy to criticise, but they had done exactly the same, even though they were on a comparatively short learning curve.

As Dorothy and Shirley were already nurses they were often sent to staff a small clinic which was run in the area. A man arrived one day with a very badly cut finger. They had some local anaesthetic so gave him an injection, pulled the skin together and stitched the wound. They gave him a shot of penicillin too. It added neatly to the experience of coping with situations when there was no doctor around.

However, they were later reproved for their action and were told, quite firmly, that they should have called the doctor to treat the patient and not tackled something so complicated themselves. It was a bit of a shock as they had felt they had handled the situation in the best possible way, especially as the doctor would have needed to come out by plane to reach them. It was a humbling time, although it proved to be the only negative comment made to them throughout the whole of jungle camp.

The final challenge was to be divided into two, and for each group to build a raft. On this they would make their journey downriver to the airstrip.

As final preparations were under way for their departure, they were given specific instructions for dealing with rubbish. Anything which would burn should be put on the fire, and then they must take great care to see that it was safely extinguished. They should dig a large hole and anything which would not burn, was to be buried carefully. It was then that

[6] *And the people grumbled and deplored their hardships, which was evil in the ears of the Lord... Number 11:1 (Amplified Bible)*

Dorothy and Shirley discovered the reason for the frequent visits of army ants. They had built their champa over a nest.

As they drifted downriver to the airstrip at the end of the camp, the expression 'Survival of the fittest' came to mind. They had survived and in general, they were fit. It was only later that Shirley discovered that she was still harbouring the bugs from her earlier bout of paratyphoid. How grateful she was that she had not been seriously ill again during jungle camp. It was sobering to reflect on the seriousness of this past three months and to wonder if the practical training of jungle camp would ever be a life-saver. Although some people had found jungle camp to be a trial, she herself had actually enjoyed the experience although a long, hot shower would certainly be very welcome!

Dorothy, Dayuma (from the Auca Indians) and Shirley

5 Wanted – a man

The contrast was startling. Less than a week before, they had been deep in thick, lush jungle but now, as they took advantage of a car ride back to Mexico city, the road wound endlessly through the dry, barren desert. The sun beat down on the car roof and the heat was stifling. The streams were completely dry and even the rivers were little more than a trickle. A few odd shrubs were dotted here and there but the most dramatic part of the landscape was the cactus plants. They were simply enormous and, when they stopped to take some photographs, the plants towered way above their heads. One particularly splendid specimen had been dubbed 'organ pipes', and for a brief moment Shirley could almost imagine herself in London's Albert Hall.

The noise, bustle and dirt of the city were also in great contrast to the previous three months. They had most certainly found plenty of dirt in the jungle and at times had wondered if they would ever be clean again, but city dirt was somehow different. Shirley was suffering from a heavy cold which was aggravated by the change of atmosphere, and her head felt like a cabbage. There was plenty to do in terms of re-packing, and a seemingly endless list of permits and visas which had to be obtained. There were those required for Peru and also for Brazil, and in general, most of the officials were courteous and helpful. Even their luggage had to have special visas from the embassy. The list of documents seemed to grow ever longer, and with it, the price. Everything seemed to be exorbitant.

Medical checks revealed that Shirley was still harbouring paratyphoid and so she needed another course of antibiotics to resolve that ongoing problem. Aside from the official paperwork, there were heaps of personal letters to catch up on too. Some rolls of developed film had arrived back in the post, but these needed to be cut and mounted into cardboard frames so that they could be used in slide presentations with interested groups of people. It all took time.

The next stage of their journey would take them via Peru to Brazil. There, language study and further acculturation awaited them. Would the training and preparation never come to an end?

The plane heading for Lima in Peru was not due to take off until the early hours of the morning. Friends from the SIL office helped them to the airport and guarded their luggage while they dealt with the official paperwork. They were considerably over their luggage limit but were grateful not to be charged excess. By the time they had taken off into the night sky there was nothing to see, and they slept on and off for a few hours. At one point they stopped at an airfield in Ecuador to refuel, before landing in Lima at lunchtime the following day. A taxi took them to their hotel and they were delighted at the luxuries which awaited them for the next twenty four hours. Even more exciting though, was the prospect of meeting up with a friend from midwifery training days. Oh – how they talked!

The hours passed all too quickly and before they knew it, the time came to board another flight for the next stage of the journey. The plane took off over the Pacific, and followed the arid Peruvian coast line for some long time before turning inland. It was extremely bumpy over the Andes and clouds obscured much of the view. The scenery gradually changed, and Shirley gazed out of the window at the miles of unbroken jungle canopy below, her thoughts lost in the future life ahead.

Rio de Janeiro was a-buzz with tourists, many of whom wanted a closer look at the statue of Christ the Redeemer overlooking the city. Standing at 130 ft tall and 98 ft wide on top of the 2300 ft Corcovado Mountain, it was certainly a breathtaking sight. Ramshackle trams loaded to capacity whizzed through the streets at breakneck speed, with dozens of people hanging on the outside.

Other visitors were heading for the famous Sugarloaf Mountain. The large granite, cone-shaped rock, rising out of the water at the entrance to Guanabara Bay, was a striking natural landmark. Sugarloaf had got its name from the unique shape which resembled a traditional form of refined sugar used in the 19th century. It was only one of the mountains around the city, with others of granite and quartz which rose straight from the water's edge.

The city itself seemed to go right down to the beach front. The sand was beautiful and the beaches were as stunning as the brochures declared them to be. On some, football and volleyball matches were in full swing, whilst on others the surfers took to the waves as the breakers roared in. Shirley was grateful to be staying high up over the city with a stunning view of the mountains. Although it was no hotter than they had been used to, the humidity was a little trying.

The tape recorder had cost a huge amount of money to get through customs, and now it was being temperamental again. It seemed as though the speed mechanism was wearing badly and it was not helped by a loose bearing. Shirley hoped that a mechanic from the Jungle Aviation and Radio Service (JAARS) would be able to give it some tender loving care. Her father continued to send tapes from England and whilst it was good to hear familiar voices, sometimes the distortion and interference made listening hard work. They were all grateful to have got their luggage through customs, as other groups had waited for up to a year for clearance.

There was not much opportunity for sight seeing and almost immediately it was time to get back to study. Although they had already touched on a number of languages including a little Spanish, it was essential for them to master Portuguese completely. Before them was an intensive three week course. Accommodation was at a premium and they were soon moved to rooms on a main road in the city itself. The noise was deafening. In writing one of her weekly letters to her father, Shirley commented on the fact that he himself had visited Rio some forty years before her. "Regarding the trams which you remember in Rio, I wouldn't be surprised if we are riding on exactly the same ones as you did 40 years ago. I often wistfully wish that I could have a few acres of jungle to get away from the noise."

Language study was intense, with no English being spoken from 8am until after the evening meal. Understanding came through actions, guesswork and a plentiful supply of artwork. They all became experts with speed and skill in drawing matchstick people to illustrate the study and communicate with each other. Whilst they understood that the theory of the teaching was to encourage them to think in Portuguese right from the start, it was easier said than done and was an exhausting process. Mealtimes were at 7am, 11.30am and 6pm and during the long afternoon session Shirley found that she often simply had to take a break away from the noise and intensity of study. Even something as simple as wandering to the local shops to buy a tube of toothpaste made a welcome break.

The time in the heart of Rio quickly came to an end and with it the need to re-pack once more. There was little time to settle. The words of scripture, "For here we have no continuing city, but we seek the one to come,"[7] seemed especially poignant. In each place they would make new friends, but then have to move on.

They gathered at the bus stop early one Saturday morning with their piles of luggage to board the 8am bus for the

[7] *Hebrews 13:14 (NKJV)*

80 mile journey to the town of Nova Friburgo, high in the mountains to the north of the Rio. It was a beautiful day and they could see for miles. The small town was also a holiday resort, nearly 3000 ft above sea level. The bus climbed slowly up the winding mountain roads.

Dorothy and Shirley had been allocated to stay with a widow who seemed delighted to have their company. She was very patient in correcting their mistakes as they murdered her language. Classes started again almost immediately, sometimes with a teacher and a local native speaker, and at other times with the local speaker alone. Shirley's helper was a 16 year old who rattled off Portuguese at an alarming speed, and both of them needed some imagination and fun to understand each other. Shirley tried to explain the learning system to her father.

"A language helper does not put up with anything that a casual listener might. The fastest method is to start with translating the language in your head but this has serious disadvantages later on. By our current method, we associate words in their context and situation and the response becomes automatic as there is no translation process. Word order is bound to be correct because we have never heard it any other way."

The town itself provided assorted interludes. There was one large main road with railway lines running down the centre. The train, although picturesque, was ancient and was powered by a wood stove which puffed out thick black smoke. A horse and cart was a popular means of transport and Shirley was rather alarmed one day to see a horse bolt after being startled by the clouds of smoke. Several people tried to stop it but both horse and cart were still going full speed when they disappeared into the distance. It was amazing that there were not more accidents, although one day a lorry collided with the top of a bus stop and a huge amount of rubble came crashing down. There was mayhem for some time as the locals tore away at piles of concrete, sadly finding the body of a child underneath.

Shops lined the street and provided everything anyone could possibly need. Houses varied hugely, from small hovels to more expensive properties and new developments around the edge of the town.

It was a delight to walk around the area. The town was built on sheer rock surrounded by mountains which were mainly covered by trees. There were numerous waterfalls which were stunningly beautiful when the sun shone on them. There were many Christian people in the town and it was always a joy to be invited out and to make new friends. On occasions Shirley and her local language helper would take a walk in the town and just chat as they went, having the language lesson on the way.

Sundays were busy with a rather lengthy service both morning and evening. Sometimes Dorothy and Shirley discovered that they had 'understood' a completely different message from each other. One Sunday all seven of the group had to stand up in the church and explain how they had come to be there. Shirley reported to her father that it had proved to be a rather grim experience. They had rehearsed their individual talks beforehand, but felt as though they were delivered parrot fashion. Most people seemed to appreciate their contributions, and they felt that perhaps they had been understood more than they thought.

The pastor of the church started to come to their Bible study groups. He was planning a trip to the States and wanted to brush up on his English. One question took them by surprise.

"Why did we sing about peas this morning?" he asked quizzically.

"Peas? Did we?" Shirley tried to stifle a chuckle as she thought through the hymns they had sung, although she realised that she was in no position to make fun of someone else.

'Yes," he continued, "peas", as he started to hum the tune.

The mystery was solved when they realised that the word was 'plea' and the pastor thereafter became 'Mr P'!

Language practice seemed never ending and bits of paper seemed to swamp them during the long days. There never seemed to be enough time to finish what they needed to do. 'Ifs' and 'buts', and 'coulds' and 'woulds' proved a challenge. Gradually though, they realised that they were gaining ground.

Communication between Shirley and her father touched on Brazilian football, troubles in Brazil, tensions in Peru, the health of Winston Churchill and less dramatic issues such as the various fruits which were available to them. Particular memories of home caught up with her from time to time. Her father had picked a rose from the garden on the morning of her departure and she had pressed the petals carefully. Every so often she would finger them gently, remembering.

The Brazil branch director visited at one point and was able to bring them up to date on the various surveys taking place from Manaus. Although there was nothing definite as to where Shirley would eventually live and work, it was good to be updated on progress and, for the first time, she was able to give her father a clue in her letters as to where she might be working. The Paumarí were a group on the south side of the Purus River. It was just a possibility at this stage that her life's work might be among them.

It was an exciting evening when they got to hear the BBC news for the first time in 14 months. How lovely to hear that staid and stately delivery of news once more. Shirley checked her watch by the 'pips' and was delighted to find that it was only two minutes out. Her birthday came round again and they were visiting a pastor and his wife on the edge of town. They did not let on that it was a special day, but were delighted when their hosts served up strawberries and cream. It seemed a really lovely touch from the Lord to make the day special, and a memory which Shirley treasured for some time.

The five months in Nova Friburgo came to an end and once more they were packing in order to return to Rio. Although it had been a comparatively short time, somehow it seemed an extra hard wrench to pull up roots and move on. On their last Sunday about 150 people turned up at the church service to send them on their way and a homily was read out by the chairman. It was so generous and enthusiastic that it almost sounded as though they had run the church, but it was, nevertheless, good to have been appreciated. Brazilian generosity was certainly something special.

The heat and humidity of the city hit them hard after the clean air of the mountains. Shirley was staying at this time with another colleague, Joyce, and their new home was with a Brazilian family on the 6th floor of an apartment block. The family had a 12 year old daughter, who often used to sit and watch Shirley as she typed. Language learning was a mutual affair as the young girl wanted to learn English.

It had been ten years since Shirley had done admin work but now, as 1962 drew to a close, she found herself in the SIL office in Rio. It seemed to work out that the job each person was given was one of which they had no previous experience. Shirley now found herself to be a cashier. The term 'filthy lucre' came to have a new meaning as some of the notes had been used so much and many of them were in the last stages of disintegration.

Firm plans for a long term assignment still seemed so far away. Surveys were ongoing as to the various indigenous groups which might be suitable, but as the time went on it became clear that it was unlikely to happen before the next conference in Rio which was due in May. Even if plans were more definite, it would be barely feasible either in terms of time or finance. In any case, there was no one else to take over in the office. The surveys were usually done by boat, but more recently a float plane had arrived from Bolivia to cut down on travel time and to reach more inaccessible places.

As the year came to a close, there was a bombshell waiting. The director called to speak to them and confirmed that the idea of going to their long term assignment was not likely to happen before the conference. That bit was not a surprise. However, he wanted them to return to Nova Friburgo and co-ordinate the next language course there until the conference. It seemed a ridiculous idea. They had barely got to grips with Portuguese themselves. There were mixed feelings as they mulled over the idea. Returning to Nova Friburgo would not be a hardship as it had become a place they were very fond of. However, the thought of supervising a Portuguese course was daunting. As Shirley continued to ponder the challenge ahead, she realised that there was a job which needed to be done. Directors and members had the same vision and by working together they would achieve their aim. It was time to start packing.

Shirley and Joyce were back in Nova Friburgo for Christmas, and booked into a hotel. To their surprise and delight a couple of colleagues had arranged for a big basket of fruit and nuts to be delivered to their room along with a vase of roses. It was the time of year for torrential downpours of rain and this year was no exception. When the skies cleared for a while they scuttled out to the shops for essential supplies and visited a few friends from their last time there. After the Christmas break they went to look at a house to rent and found something which was fully furnished. It was slightly bigger than they needed and at a higher rent too, but in the end they decided to take it.

In addition to the anticipation of running the course, they now found themselves running a house. It was quite old and they soon discovered that it had some idiosyncrasies. When it rained heavily – which it did frequently – the water came in around the windows and under the door. The house owner had previously installed a tank underground, with a pump to get water into the property. But there was no way of knowing when it was empty and if it ran dry it meant an airlock in the pipe which supplied the bath. They became quite adept at removing the tap from the wall in order to remedy the matter.

There was a gas leak in the kitchen stove. With the price of gas cylinders just having risen, they were reluctant to let gas escape constantly, quite apart from the safety hazard. A man eventually came to look at it and although not 100% it was certainly better than before. As the days went by the frustrations mounted. A letter home read as follows:

Wanted – A man!

"*Running the Portuguese course may be a job that two single girls can manage, however, after a three month experiment we have reached the conclusion that running a house isn't. Maybe we should say, running the repairs of a house. Anyway, whichever way you look at it the repairs keep us running.*

"*Let us start in the feminine domain – the kitchen. The gas taps leak badly and having brought no tools, we need a man. Unless the sink gets regular attention we are sunk – we need a man.*

"*The bathroom provides an interesting feature. Once in a while the pipes get air-locked and we get no water. To remove this minor defect there is the simple remedy of removing the tap (faucet) from the wall, by which method one can have two simultaneous showers immediately. With one hand over the hole in the wall the plug is gradually manipulated back into place by which time the manipulator has had her shower.*

"*Then, in the living room all is in turmoil. Outside it is raining heavily. Inside, a row of buckets, bowls and saucepans are collecting the water which is pouring through a colander-like ceiling. For the umpteenth time we plead for a man to remove the leaves from the gutters above. There was of course the little matter of the outside drain, which didn't. One man came and went and then another, but the dirty water still remained to pervade the garden with an unusual perfume. Finally, after much persuasion, we got a man who drained the drain.*

"Troubles over? Not yet. For one man who had failed to drain the drain succeeded in turning off our incoming water supply. What better time than the tea break on a half day of prayer to discover that there is not a drop of water in the "tank that never runs dry"? This time we had some men to lift a concrete slab and peer into its murky depths. We now have an abundance of water in the outside tank, but the pump has decided...not to! A man, we need a man, a man with tools, a man with time, we scour the town for such a man to put our motor right. What better time to be without water when you have visitors for the weekend? With all hands mobilised, five single girls carried the water from those murky depths to fill every vessel that could be found.

"By having visitors we discovered a broken leg on the unused bed. We found a man who 'volunteered' to put that right, but failed to find a man with a saw to lend to the man who put it right!

"The garden of course we do not touch. We are cultivating our own little jungle for lack of a man to pull up the weeds and prune back the rest.

"When we have finished running the repairs, we may even find time to run the course, but in the meantime we have perfected a Portuguese phrase... "Nós precisamos de um homen... **We need a man!"**

Thunderstorms in Nova Friburgo were dramatic, as the lights in the house flicked and dimmed during the storm. The noise of the thunder echoed around the mountains.

The price of electricity shot up and many people were finding times hard. Beggars often came knocking on the door but the ladies were reluctant to give money, knowing that it would probably be spent on drink. A gift of food seemed a better option. At the market they were gradually learning how to pick out corn which was young and fresh, the names of fruit and vegetables and how to choose a juicy pineapple.

Carnival time was approaching, an annual festival in Brazil which lasted for a week just before Lent, with festivities going on night and day. There was generally a huge consumption of beer during this time, and it was not considered safe for women to be out alone at night. The custom had also evolved that on Ash Wednesday, when the celebrations finally ceased, the people would go to church for confession.

There were some sobering moments in the weeks before Easter. A 13 year old boy was run over by the ancient train in the main road, and his death cast a shadow over the town. In addition, news came through of two Wycliffe members who had been killed by guerrillas in Vietnam.

Back in Rio for the conference, Shirley was looking forward to further news on her long term assignment. Each evening there were reports from members working with different indigenous groups, although for some, the work of translation was in its very early stages. Two groups with reputations for savagery had been contacted with the teams involved giving wonderful testimonies of what God had done for them during this time. They planned to go back and make further attempts at peaceful contacts. It seemed as though there had been some very unfortunate incidents with outsiders in the past, and it was no wonder that they treated any further contact with suspicion or open warfare.

It had now been two years since Shirley had stepped off the SS United States and onto American soil and yet, as the conference came to its conclusion, it was still not clear where she was to go. Two years of training, more training, language study, jungle camp, packing, unpacking, making friends and saying 'Goodbye'. Once more, however, there was a job to be done and someone needed to do it. So it was that Shirley found herself going to the Apinajé village to cover the work of a member who was on home leave. It meant settling down to study yet another language.

The six months in the village was a temporary assignment although as the weeks passed, Shirley would have been happy to stay with this community who she quickly grew to appreciate and respect.

Back in Rio as 1963 drew to a close, Shirley studied the survey reports. For some long time she had considered and prayed about who she should work with once her assignment was clear, and Mary Ann Odmark seemed to be the right one. They did not know each other well and indeed, all she knew about Mary Ann was that she was American from a town in the north near to the Canadian border. Together they looked at the comments about each indigenous group of people – where they lived, how many there were in each village, what language they already spoke and other general comments. As they discussed the various options with the mission director, the answer became clear. They would go to the Paumarí.

Much of the previous practical training now swung into action as they prepared lists and started to pack. There would be a brief stop in Manaus for more shopping and from there, for three months they would be completely cut off from the world. This was no time to forget something important.

6 Early days

As the single engine Norseman flew over the tree tops, Shirley gazed out of the window. Mary Ann was sitting beside her, and every so often they exchanged a few words or pointed out something interesting, but it was hard to talk over the noise of the engine. In any case, the view was mostly of tree tops and more tree tops from the thick jungle below them. From time to time they caught sight of the Purus River. Although not so well known as the mighty Amazon, it is a tributary of that majestic waterway which floods much of the jungle floor for several months each year. The Purus is one of the most winding rivers in the world, with loop after loop meandering through the jungle. When it came into view through the thick canopy of foliage, the sun reflected off the water like diamonds on a tiara. Just occasionally they caught sight of a wisp of smoke as it lazily curled skywards from an isolated settlement.

It was a five hour flight from Manaus, and there was plenty of time to reflect. Shirley's mind had been so full of shopping lists for this first session in the village and she wondered, for the umpteenth time, if she had forgotten anything important. She reflected on others who had made similar journeys. Her mind went back to the group who had ventured into Auca territory in Ecuador less than ten years previously, full of vision and enthusiasm just like she was now. But within days, five of them had been killed on the beach there in the village. She thought of the Auca lady she had met back in Sulphur Springs, and wondered where Dayuma was now.

Her thoughts went back to particular moments of her own surrender to God. Each one had been a powerful experience, but what did the future hold for her now among the

Paumarí? How would they react to two single white women coming to live among them? There was no way of knowing.

She had studied the survey reports of the area and knew that the Paumarí lived on the edge of Lake Maraha. The whole geography of the area, however, changed so much with the seasons. Over time, some of the loops from the Purus had become cut off from the main river to become lakes. Indeed, in the dry season they could be classified as oxbow lakes, with just the smallest trickle of water connecting them to the main river, whilst in the wet season there was a deeper attachment. Shirley knew that there were three groups of Paumarí, but the village to which she and Mary Ann were now heading belonged to the group who lived at the furthest edge of an oxbow lake, about three miles from the main river. She had studied the surveys with such care and guessed that the lake was about half a mile wide. She wondered if she would recognise the village from the air.

Her stomach turned over from time to time. Although by now she had worked in a number of villages with other colleagues, each of them had some contact with the outside world, even if it was just the occasional horse or mule being led along a road. The Paumarí village was different. There was no road. There was no air strip. There were no shops. There was no electricity, running water or sanitation. Their only contact would be with river traders and local inhabitants. There were no two-way radios. Once the pilot took off to return to Manaus, she and Mary Ann would be on their own. They had with them a small transistor radio and hoped to pick up some messages which they knew were broadcast to people in the area. The battery power, however, was a fragile resource and in any case, they had no idea if they would get a decent reception on it. As for contact from them to anyone else, there would be nothing at all. For three months they were on their own. The Paumarí would be their neighbours, and she hoped that they might also become friends.

Mixed in with the apprehension was anticipation. This was the moment she had dreamed of for so many years since she first knew that God had called her to serve Him in South America. She had thought back then that it would be as a nurse, but now it seemed as though she would be a translator. She had touched on some Spanish and several languages from the various villages where she had worked, but within a very short time she must communicate with these people who had nothing written down. She had learnt Portuguese and could speak it reasonably well. She and the Paumarí would have to muddle along with what they knew of Portuguese between them, until she could get to grips with their own language.

It seemed unfair to call them illiterate – although they were – as they had never had a written language. She would have to learn to speak their language and then work out the best way to write it before she could even start to translate the scriptures for them. Somewhere in the equation she would need to teach them to read their own language. What a task! She wondered, as she had many times before, if she was up to the job. As her stomach continued to churn with apprehension and anticipation, there was also the usual travel sickness thrown in too. She would not be sorry when they touched down and she could step out onto solid ground once more.

Excitement began to rise within her as she realised that they were nearly there, and the pilot called out to them to confirm this. She had rehearsed in her mind dozens of times what she planned to say as her introduction to the Paumarí and now spoke it over silently for a last practice. She scoured the horizon for a glimpse of the lake – and suddenly there it was! There was no more time to be scared. This was the moment they had been waiting for. As the pilot circled the lake they could see the villagers coming out of their houses to stare into the sky. She guessed that they would never have seen a plane close up before. She caught sight of a few small children who clung to their mother's skirts. The plane would be an awesome sight for them, and she knew that this was an historic moment both for her, and for them.

They had been flying comparatively low at 5000 feet so the descent did not take long. The pilot now skilfully brought the float plane down and it skimmed over the surface of the lake before coming to a stop somewhere in the middle. He then taxied slowly to the edge. Shirley and Mary Ann remained seated while he shut off the engine and opened the door. He stepped out and waited to help his passengers. There was one fixed step and from there, a slightly tricky manoeuvre to stand on the float as the plane rocked with the movement. As they edged along the float, they would then step onto anything on the land which appeared reasonably firm.

As the pilot busied himself securing the plane, some of the villagers edged a little closer, but they seemed very apprehensive. The children's faces showed both fear and fascination. Shirley and Mary Ann gave their greetings in Portuguese and were relieved when they seemed to be reciprocated. The pilot helped them to make small talk, all the while keeping a close watch on the children, some of whom were, by now, in the water, touching the plane as they chattered amongst themselves.

The houses, such as they were, stood on stilts about three feet off the ground with a notched log acting as steps. There were five or six of them in a row near the water's edge. They were extremely basic structures and most did not have walls. They were devoid of furniture. In general it seemed as though the main living area was open on all sides. A small area seemed to be slightly lower than the rest and Shirley guessed that this was for cooking. The house was completed with a leafy roof. It looked as though families did everything together, and in full view of everyone else. The life style was rather daunting, but Shirley and Mary Ann knew that if they were to be accepted by these people, they would have to live like them as much as possible.

She turned to one of the men who seemed to be taking a lead in the introductions, and asked if it would be possible for him to build them a house. It was only much later that she discovered that in doing so she had committed a major faux-pas. Perhaps it was just as well that she did not realise it at the time. After all her training in culture, she would have been mortified to have offended him in some way, especially having only just stepped into his village. When she did learn the truth it was to discover that the men only ever built houses for their wives – not for strange single women who had only just arrived! Fortunately, however, the man let the mistake pass, and a group of them suggested that she could buy a house. They pointed one out to her and said that the owner was away. This in itself seemed to be a precarious arrangement and fraught with misunderstandings, but they finally persuaded the ladies that the owner would be agreeable to the idea.

The pilot had started to unload the plane and he now looked to the men and older children as if to ask for their help. He had realised that they would not touch something which belonged to another person for fear of being accused of stealing, but were more than happy to help if they were invited. Once that cultural nicety was out of the way, it was 'all hands on deck' as almost everyone got involved in handing the drums and all the other boxes and cases over the water to the dry land. Some of the children tried to roll the drums up the first steep part of the bank although they needed some adult help to get the momentum going. Once on the level ground, however, the drums rolled easily and before they knew it, the luggage was all taken up into the house. Many of the villagers came too.

The main floor of the house was about ten feet square.
Shirley and Mary Ann, tired from their flight, now found
themselves entertaining almost the entire village. Their
luggage took up a lot of space but it was apparent that
the villagers were not going to miss a moment of this
extraordinary event. They had clearly not had so much fun
in a long time. As Shirley quickly realised that her whole
life was going to remain under constant scrutiny from this
moment on, she decided to make a start at unpacking. It was
a time consuming affair as each item was examined carefully
and passed around from one to another. She felt alienated
from the process as they spoke to each other in Paumarí
but, nevertheless, it proved to be a useful bonding session.
Everyone sat on the floor or on their haunches and no one
was in a hurry to go anywhere.

Some of the men offered some firewood and the pilot got
a small fire going. It was a little awkward to cook with the
rest of the village watching, although by now some of them
had retreated to their own houses, popping back every few
minutes to make sure that they were not missing anything
exciting. It seemed that the pressure lamp caused a great stir.

As night fell that first evening, Shirley and Mary Ann realised
the urgency of getting some water from the lake. They had
a bucket and took a torch as they made their way gingerly
down the log which acted as steps from the house. They
wanted to collect some water away from the edge of the lake
in the hope that it might be a little bit cleaner out there, and
planned on using any canoe which they could find. There
were indeed two tied up which were resting on a sloping
part of the bank, but both were full of water.

They used the bucket to bail one of them out until it was
half full, and then pushed off from the shore. But the canoe
was still too full to float and was quickly going down.
Instinct kicked in to them both at the same moment – jump

into the other canoe. That sank too! It was some while before they finally made their way back to the house, soaking wet but with their precious water. Many of the villagers were still waiting there and Shirley hoped that the darkness had obscured some of their exploits. They did appreciate, however, that they would be the main source of entertainment for a long time to come!

Their uninvited guests continued to stay. Shirley and Mary Ann found their air beds and got them filled and ready. They also unpacked the mosquito nets and managed to rig them up sufficiently for the first night. It felt very strange to have every move watched so closely and still the villagers remained where they were. Shirley and Mary Ann had not rehearsed the cultural issue of getting people to leave. They spoke to each other in English and eventually they made moves to extinguish the light. Only then did they realise that it was the pressure lamp which was causing such late night fascination. The people wanted to see how they put it out. Once that was done, they took their cue and departed. The pilot left as well, to sleep in one of the Paumarí houses.

Shirley and Mary Ann were exhausted, but their minds were too full of the day's events for them to sleep. It felt very strange to be so exposed to the whole village. Eventually, however, the night-time sounds of the jungle lulled them off to a fitful sleep.

As light came with the dawn around 6am the next morning, the ladies watched as the Paumarí began a new day. A steep learning curve had begun. They had realised the night before that the only toilet facility was the jungle itself. Some people had gone down to the lake to wash; and others got fires going outside their houses. Some of the men were already out fishing.

The first twenty four hours passed in a bit of a daze. The pilot set to work to build them a mud stove and he too had a constant audience. There was plenty to do and it was hard to know where to start. It was important to communicate with the people as much as possible and as a result, every task took extra time as they tried to make conversation in broken Portuguese. But both Shirley and Mary Ann appreciated that in these early days it was vital to make a start at earning respect and trust. It was going to be a two-way challenge. There was still plenty left to unpack, but it was hard to know how to store their supplies in such a small space.

It was hot and sticky, and by lunchtime they were more than ready for a swim. Several of the women and children were in the water. There was a raft house tethered just a short distance from the shore and most people seemed to take a canoe to it and swim from there. Shirley did not understand why they did this as the children splashed around at the water's edge, but she decided to follow the local custom. She paused for a few moments to watch the children swimming. They were like fish and it was fascinating to watch them dive under and then pop up in the most unexpected places. There was still caution about these strange ladies, and both parents and children were clearly a little apprehensive.

They were awake early again the following morning. The pilot was already up and keen to be on his way back to Manaus. This was the moment Shirley had been dreading. She and Mary Ann walked with him back down to the edge of the water, followed by a trail of villagers. He untied the plane and made his final preparations. He gave them a word of encouragement and said goodbye to the watching crowd. Shirley knew that tears were threatening but she dare not let them come. He closed the door and started the engine.

As he manoeuvred into the right position, he revved the engine and it roared more loudly. Some of the children put their hands over their ears. The water churned as the pilot accelerated and they watched silently as the plane gathered speed down the length of the lake. Shirley struggled to contain her emotions as the aircraft rose above the water and disappeared over the tree tops.

There was only one word which could sum up her feelings at that moment. Abandonment. Although she was with Mary Ann and although it was already very clear that they would seldom be alone, she felt bereft. In her spirit she knew that God would never leave her or forsake her, but just at that moment her spirit was outnumbered by body, mind and emotions which all screamed at her that she was out of contact and totally isolated.

As she turned slowly to walk back to the house she just longed for somewhere private where she could go and have a good cry. But there was nowhere private in this place. Her whole life would now be on display from sunrise to sunset. It was a scary prospect and she wondered how she would ever cope. Even now a stream of people followed them back and sat, watching. She could sense from their reactions that they were surprised. She guessed that they had expected her to stay one night and then step back into the plane the next morning. Perhaps it was as well that they did not know how much she had longed to do just that.

Later that day they unpacked the pressure cooker which provoked a great deal of interest and the women edged as near as they dared to inspect it more closely. They were more than a little scared of it. Some of them tried to frighten their children about the new ladies who had come to the village and told them that Shirley and Mary Ann would cook them in their pot! The children, however, were quickly beginning to warm to these visitors and seemed to be much more realistic than their parents. They treated the threats with the contempt they deserved.

Some of the men approached later to offer some fish. It seemed to be another custom to offer first rather than risk the shame of a gift having been rejected. The ladies certainly did not want to refuse and accepted gratefully.

The village was small, with just seven houses. These were built quite closely together. One of them was considerably bigger than the rest and was known – not surprisingly – as The Big House. Shirley tried to count the number of people in the village. Over some time she guessed she had seen around one hundred different people, but there were lots of coming and goings so it was hard to tell who was who.

It was fortunate that it was the dry season and they could walk around. They knew that as the waters rose later in the year the whole village would be flooded, and then every trip anywhere would have to be made by canoe. Research had shown them that for approximately three months of the year the water in the lake was at its lowest, for three months the waters were rising, for about the next three months it was flooded and for the other three months the waters receded. A lot depended, however, on the amount of snow melting on the Andes. It would be interesting – and challenging – to live entirely on the water. What did one do about toilet needs, she wondered, when there was nowhere to go? It was good that they did not have to meet that problem just yet. The thought crossed her mind that there was one advantage to being so close to the water. When the lake was flooded the pilot would be able to come right to the front door. It would be very different from getting to an airport on time. At this stage, however, it was hard to imagine.

Shirley could see into the other houses from where she lived and it seemed as though almost everything happened there on the raised floor. A mother might be swinging her toddler in a hammock from time to time, while at the same time stripping the fronds of the açaí fruit. She would then leave them in a bowl of hot water for a while to soften the skin, while she did some other task. After a while she would put her hands into the bowl with the mushy mixture of fruit and would swirl it around to loosen the stones. With just the skin and fruit left, the remaining mixture was sieved, with the juice being the main result. When Shirley and Mary Ann were offered some, they generally boiled it before drinking it, but even so, it did not keep for long. It was delicious, but quickly went sour. It was not hard to see why the children so often had a purple stain around their mouths.

The children ran around barefoot and seemed oblivious to the hard ground. They often went naked. From a small age the boys seemed to weald large knives with complete control. It was stomach churning at first to see them cut open a delicate stem with a knife about 12 inches long, but it seemed like second nature to them. Even young ones shinned up the tall palm trees quicker than you could say 'coconut', with machete swinging as they went.

Over those first few days Shirley began to see the process of making farinha. This was the staple diet of the people, and was prepared from the root of the manioc plant. The process was long and complicated. She could see an old canoe which had been filled with soaking manioc roots and then left to sit in the hot sun for a few days. She was slightly shocked when the roots began to rot, but the villagers did not seem to be concerned.

After several days she watched as they picked up a root and saw that the outer skin dropped off in one piece. They squashed down the remaining root to squeeze out some of the water which contained cyanide, and then put it in a manioc press to force out even more of the liquid. Then they sieved the remaining substance to get rid of the fibres. At that stage, they produced a huge pan which seemed to be about six feet across. It was the biggest Shirley had ever seen. They had built a support frame for it and got a fire going underneath, and then toasted the prepared manioc in the pan, turning it over and over so that the remaining moisture could evaporate.

Once dry, the yellow deposit was taken out and left to cool in cloth sacks. It was then stored in special baskets which had been lined with large leaves. So this was farinha! She would become very familiar with it in days to come. It was hard to describe farinha. It looked like gravel, but tasted like nothing in particular. It was difficult to eat dry and was much better when used to mop up the juice from boiled fish or meat.

In time, Shirley noted an alternative method of preparing it which was also used for the sweet variety of manioc. They had an old tin through which they had banged some nails to make a sort of grater. After peeling off the outer skin they grated the root, washed and toasted it, and then what had settled in the washing process was actually tapioca flour.

The Paumarí had grown up with a history of massacre. The story they recounted started off as history and concluded as mythical events. They had a deep mistrust of non-indigenous people who would often come through the village.

"Aren't you scared of them?" they sometimes asked of Shirley and Mary Ann.

These visitors were equally scared of the Paumarí and asked the same question.

As the days went by Shirley and Mary Ann were grateful for every small gesture of acceptance which was shown to them. The villagers often offered them food. Sometimes it was chunks of fish or turtle meat, and at other times hands and arms which looked as though they might have come from monkeys. Fish was a large part of the diet and if there was no food around once the family had woken in the morning, then the man of the house would go out in a canoe to catch some.

The children gradually became less timid and it was a special day when the first one climbed up on Shirley's lap. All the

women breast-fed their babies and were quite willing to
baby-sit and feed a child for an absent mother. Shirley was
concerned about toddlers falling off the raised floor of the
houses, although there did not seem to be many accidents.
Parakeets, parrots and other pets often sat on the communal
living area.

Shirley and Mary Ann soon decided that living in such a
public arena themselves was going to be hard work, and
they asked some of the men if they would make palm leaf
walls for the house. Tall screens at the back and sides made
a huge difference, and an inner wall made a bedroom
separate from the living area, giving them some privacy.
They also added a small low wall at the front and a half door.
It was a great improvement. A small table and a couple of
benches were a very useful addition too. Some way away
from the house, at the edge of the jungle, the men fenced
off a small area and dug them a hole in the ground. The mod
cons now knew no bounds!

The loud screaming had been going on for several hours.
Shirley guessed that one of the women was in labour and all
her instincts called for her to go and see if she could help.
Another part of her told her to hold back and not to push in
too soon in this culture where traditional methods had been
dominant for generations.

"My baby is dead and I am going to die too." The woman
continued to wail, hour after hour. During the surveys which
had been done in the area word had got out that Shirley was
a nurse and so, eventually, she was asked to go and help.
The woman could not be pacified, even though Shirley tried
to reassure her that the baby's heart beat was good and
strong, and that there was no reason why she should not be
delivered safely.

However, as the time went by repeated examinations
showed that the birth was not progressing as it should be.

The only medicine that Shirley had which could possibly help was one ampoule of morphine. 'To give or not to give, that was the question.' She had no antidote. If she gave the morphine to help the woman's pain and the baby came quickly then all was well, but if labour still did not progress, then the drug might affect the baby. But as the baby's heart beat began to get a little erratic, she felt that she had no choice. The effect was incredible. The woman began to push almost immediately. Until that moment the husband and other male relatives had sat outside the mosquito net but now, to Shirley's horror, they all crowded in. To add to her shock, the men who were present now began to gather round and press on the woman's abdomen.

Shirley cried out to them to stop, but before she knew what was happening, the poor little mite shot out like a cannon ball. It was pale and limp, and did not cry. Shirley gathered it up and started resuscitation. She also clamped the cord in two places and cut between them. The Paumarí were horrified. They had never seen clamps before and thought that they were scissors. It was their turn to shout at Shirley, saying that the baby would bleed to death. They were equally horrified when she turned the baby upside down by the ankles to try and get it to start breathing. Shirley took the baby back into her lap and started artificial respiration. Time was running out.

Just then, she was soaked in cold water from head to foot. It appeared that their custom was to pour cold water over a newborn to stimulate breathing, and with Shirley in the way, she got doused as well. The moments passed and eventually the baby let out a tiny wail. It was a weak cry, but it was enough. Shirley breathed a sigh of relief. It did not bear thinking about for the baby to die on her first delivery in the village. She herself was shocked at what she had witnessed and retreated as soon as was appropriate so that the family could care for mother and baby in their own traditional way.

For a moment her mind flashed back ruefully to that first delivery on her own as a student in London's East End. She wondered what her mentor might have said had she been in the village today.

In the early days it was hard to think much about language study. Daily living provided some basic vocabulary, but it was difficult to remember a word when she could not see it written. The humidity was clearly going to take its toll on the typewriter, and even after a few days the keys began to have a mouldy look about them.

Life, however, began to settle into some sort of routine. The Paumarí, whose lifestyle was simple and devoid of modern technology, began to accept the two white women who had come to live among them. They were a great help as Shirley and Mary Ann adjusted to the isolation and culture of the village, and helped in all sorts of ways, both practically and in teaching them new words. It was perhaps another gesture of acceptance when the villagers decided that Shirley and Mary Ann needed some pets. So it was that their tiny house had two more residents – Buster and Rosa.

Shirley and Mary Ann's first house

Midwife Shirley

7 House guests

The expression 'What a mangy looking dog', took on a new meaning in the village. Many of the dogs which roamed around under the houses were very poor looking specimens. Infected with contagious parasitic mites, their fur was often threadbare and their bones stuck out through scabby, unhealthy skin. They were a thoroughly miserable sight.

Buster, however, was in a class above the rest! He was a real 'Heinz 57' breed of dog and was a present from the Paumarí to Mary Ann. He made it clear from the start that he had no intention of living life under the house. His place was with the ladies in their tiny abode. Like most of the dogs in the village, his personality was something of a mixture between pig and vulture. He was, however, extremely useful in eating up any scraps which the ladies passed to him under the table. It would have been very rude to refuse any gifts of food which were given to them, but some of the larger fish were extremely greasy and very hard to digest. Even the Paumarí preferred the smaller ones. But in that environment one could not be too fussy, and if the larger ones were the only ones which were available, then that was on the menu. Buster had no qualms about fatty fish. He would eat anything and on occasions it was useful to surreptitiously pass him the scraps. With Shirley's medical knowledge he had his own private health care service. He thrived.

One day there was a disturbance with a broody hen. Buster had been stealing her eggs but had been caught in the act by Mary Ann as he took the last one. She had rescued it just in time, but the shell was badly cracked. She mended it with sticky tape but they did not hold out much hope of the chick surviving this early crisis in its life. However, the disturbance proved to be the result of the hen trying to get the chick out of the shell. It had indeed survived and was ready to hatch, but breaking its way out through sticky tape was more than it could manage. Mary Ann went to the rescue once more and removed the tape. Out popped a new chick! It was a strange looking creature like its mother, with no feathers on its neck and looking a little more like a feather duster than a hen.

Buster did not like the vampire bats. He got bitten and clearly did not feel so well. Some Paumarí ladies helped his two loving veterinary nurses to rig up a box for him with netting on the sides, but he did not realise that he should not put his feet against the net and so he promptly got bitten again the next night. He was really groggy for a couple of days. They went back to the drawing board and designed a further bat-proof box which seemed to do the trick. Shirley worried that it was almost air-tight by now and it was certainly a tight fit as he was getting quite sizeable, but he went in quite happily. They had to assume from his heavy breathing that he was sleeping soundly!

One of Buster's favourite pastimes was to chase pigs. Around the village a number of pigs roamed at will and no one in particular seemed to own them. Sometimes they took to sleeping under Shirley and Mary Ann's house, but when they woke and decided to scratch themselves on the supporting poles, it was as though an earthquake had struck. Buster discovered the joy of chasing them away.

The pigs were very destructive to a clump of banana plants which were just outside the house. They cut through the stem to chew on the juicy base and to bring down the unripe bananas. Buster took it upon himself to be guard dog to the banana plants.

Shirley's gift from the Paumarí was a green parrot who they called Rosa. She was just sprouting her first feathers. Rosa made herself at home but was extremely nosey and soon had her beak into everything. Shirley developed the technique of picking Rosa up across her shoulders and carrying her, feet in the air and squawking noisily, to somewhere she could do no mischief. After a while she seemed to enjoy this mode of transport and surrendered happily, even seeming to enjoy the ride.

The days were busy and always hot and humid. It was 90° F by around 10 am and the fierce heat remained until late afternoon. The sheer practicalities of living took up a huge amount of time and it was frustrating to see the days and weeks slip past without any quality time for language study. As the Paumarí became more confident with their new neighbours, more and more of them came to ask for medical help. There also seemed to be a steady stream of other people who lived in the area. It was so time consuming to be treating an endless queue of patients. Some said that they had travelled for several days to get her help, so what else could she do but attend to them as best she could? She tried to say that she would only receive non-Paumarí on Saturdays, but if a patient was really sick when they arrived there was no way they could be left. If they arrived on any other day, this presented different problems. The Paumarí would not speak their language in front of these non-Paumarí visitors and did not like to have them in their houses. Shirley was also concerned what diseases they might actually be bringing into the village with them.

In terms of language study it felt to Shirley as though she was tackling a 10,000 piece jigsaw puzzle in her brain. Sometimes her mind would return to her vision - to bring the scriptures to the Paumarí people in their own language - but the task was immense. From time to time she would close her eyes and imagine the picture on her metaphoric jigsaw. The deep longing in her heart was that one day, she would hold in her hands the completed New Testament, and be able to give it to these people who were now sharing their lives with her. But at this stage she felt as though she was just shuffling a few jigsaw pieces around. Occasionally, some came together, and those days were special indeed.

Shirley had heard it said that the indigenous languages were deficient, but she began to realise that language and culture were closely linked. Why would they need words such as cement-mixer, traffic lights, refrigerator, railway carriage etc when these words had no place at all in their culture? In truth, their language was both beautiful and complex. The verb 'to fall' for example, had a different word depending on a number of things – falling onto land was different from falling into the water; there was another word if it was describing one object which was falling and yet another word to describe something like a bunch of fruit falling. There was yet another distinction between something falling over on the land and something which might have fallen out of a canoe. So a single verb had a group of 'jigsaw pieces' which she could piece together as a tiny part of the whole.

Another small section was the verb of motion, to 'come' and 'go'. There was an obligatory difference between the word for come on the land or on water, with another for go on the land and another for go on the water. 'Bring' and 'take' were also part of the verb of motion. It was impossible to use this verb without specifying whether it was on land or water, coming or going.

The Paumarí did not have a word for 'ant'. That is to say, they did not have one word, but a separate word for every kind of ant. Similarly, they had a new word for every kind of fish, for every kind of monkey and so on.

As Shirley and Mary Ann delved into the language, the more they realised how much they had to learn. The Paumarí were willing teachers but their own command of the language was highly skilled and it was hard to keep up with their thoughts. If, for example, Shirley held out her hand to ask for the appropriate word, they might think she wanted the word for 'hand' or for 'fingers' or that she was asking them to give her something. If the meaning was not clear on the first attempt they would change the word order with amazing speed, at which point she was hopelessly lost.

Shirley and Mary Ann knew that it was important to analyse the sound system, so that they could prepare an alphabet which reflected the significant sounds, that is, those which the Paumarí could distinguish as being different. The Paumarí only heard three different vowels even though they used many more. Unlike English, however, they had two different 'b' and 'd' sounds which needed to be written differently, so that they would be able to read them correctly. It was also important to understand the way that the grammar system worked. Changes in the order of words and the subsequent change of gender agreements were complicated. Speakers could not explain why they rearranged the word order, and what those changes signalled.

The analysis of the grammar was a challenge that would take several years to piece together. As their vocabulary increased, it became necessary to start compiling a dictionary. Each new word with the guessed meaning was written on a small card, and filed. It was a long and arduous process, but without a good understanding of the way in which the language worked, they knew that they would never get to grips with an accurate and meaningful translation. However, their studies were constantly interrupted by the arrival of people needing medical help or with numerous other requests.

In addition, they needed to understand the culture, values and beliefs in order to press on with their work. It was also vitally important to understand the kinship system. The concept of aunt and uncle was not the same as it might be in other cultures. A mother's sister, for example, would also be called mother, but a father's sister would be called an aunt. Other family members also had different titles to those they were familiar with.

In Paumarí, there was a different word for an older brother or a younger brother. Shirley realised that in translation this would pose a problem. James and John were brothers, Andrew and Peter were brothers, Mary and Martha were sisters. But the Bible did not say exactly who was the older in each case, although they could take a shrewd guess.

The villagers sometimes took a canoe and went across the lake to where the main river passed by. River traders came along here and they conducted any business with them on a bartering system. The Paumarí were very enthusiastic when Shirley and Mary Ann introduced the idea of them being paid for any work which they did for the ladies, and especially as they were to be paid with real money. They had often felt exploited by the local land owner, although whether he deliberately cheated them or simply could not add up was hard to tell. He was, however, not best pleased when Mary Ann challenged his maths.

The Paumarí were very keen to learn arithmetic and so maths lessons were introduced even before reading. A group would arrive every evening to learn. The villagers had an unconventional approach to counting. One, two, three, four and five were fine. After that they spoke of two hands, and if necessary, one foot and another foot. So Shirley had to adapt her teaching to allow for their understanding and the limitations of their numbering system. For that reason learning maths in Portuguese proved to be the most practical.

In terms of learning the Paumarí language, Shirley and Mary Ann felt as though they were all learning together. They would hear a new word and write it down phonetically until they had time to work out the best way to spell it.

As the villagers became more accustomed to the ladies living with them, they slowly began to break down the reserves of caution, and friendships began to develop. Some of the Paumarí confessed to Shirley one day that before she came they had heard rumours about these strange white ladies. They had been told that if they did not learn to read their own language within two weeks, Shirley was going to cut their tongues out! They were able to laugh together.

Time seemed to have a meaning all of its own in the village. In some ways the weeks sped past with incredible speed, but in other ways they were so cut off from civilisation that it felt as though they were light years away. Shirley continued to write to her father as often as she could, usually as a long letter to which she added news as and when she had spare moments. She looked forward to the day when she would hear some news back from him about family and friends, and be able to send something to him in return.

The plan was for them to stay in the village for three months at a time, and then to return to Manaus for about six weeks. During that time they would be able to consolidate some of their language study without incessant interruptions, replenish stocks of food and medical supplies and generally gather strength for the next stretch in the village. It would be a real luxury to be clean for a while too. At that stage there was no official SIL centre in Manaus and they would need to stay in the home of the pilot or anyone else willing and able to take them in. Although they had an expected date of when the pilot would come for them, it could be dependent on many things, not least the weather. Just once in a while a plane would pass by at high altitude, and this was usually from the Brazilian air force or a commercial airliner. Their own pilot would occasionally fly over on his way to another village but it was always a special moment when they heard the sound of the Norseman coming for them.

Once a week, a radio station in Manaus broadcast messages for people living in the interior. The local SIL manager would send a message to all the teams. It was always a time of great anticipation.

"Attention all linguists... attention all linguists..." Each message was given three times with short intervals between. Interference from other channels was always a problem and if they were not able to understand the message the first time they would get out the tape recorder and have it running ready to record the second or third announcement. But even this often proved a technical nightmare. Firstly, there had to be adequate reception and sufficient battery power on the radio. Then they were dependent on the tape recorder working and enough battery power in that too. Even then, the reception was often of variable quality.

But an additional complication was that Shirley and Mary Ann were never alone during the daylight hours, and the Paumarí did not seem to understand that it was imperative that they keep quiet for those precious moments when a message was being broadcast. If there was no message for them, or it they missed it for whatever reason, it would be another week before there was another chance. The radio broadcast might give them a clue as to some world event, but in general they needed to conserve battery power for essential messages.

Battery power was often a problem in other ways too. They learned the hard way that batteries could often be half dead when they bought them and this was not only a nuisance but added considerable expense. Eventually they bought a battery tester and would check all the new batteries before they left the shop. As they bought several boxes of 24 batteries at a time, the shop keeper could hardly complain as he wanted their custom.

Rewinding tapes used a lot of battery power and Shirley often turned them by hand in order to save the precious resource. It was a thoroughly tedious process though, and she would often grab anything which was to hand to make the job just a little bit quicker.

Fishing was an important skill in the village and the boys learnt from an early age, starting with a pliable stick. They quickly progressed to using bows and arrows like the men, often standing on the edge of a canoe out in the lake. The men constructed harpoons on a pole 6-8 feet long. They would flatten and sharpen a nail, carving barbs into it, and then fixed it to the end of a small stick. This was then attached to the longer pole. At other times they used nets. There were so many different techniques. Sometimes the Paumarí would extract some poison from a particular type of vine, which they then used in small streams to paralyse the fish. Once they had come to the surface of the water they were easy enough to catch, and the poison did not seem to affect the quality of the meat. Sometimes the fish were even caught by hand in the roots of trees standing in shallow water. However, that could also be a hiding place for a snake or electric eel. Traps were also set at strategic locations.

From time to time Shirley and Mary Ann tried their hand at fishing, although the little boys often seemed to be more skilled than them. On one occasion they had been trying for some time with fish hook and stick, moving around the lake to different locations, but still without success. Suddenly, a fish which was about 12 inches long jumped straight into the canoe, and both of them dived for it at the same moment. Shirley was out in the canoe alone one day when she grabbed a small fish, but a sharp spike got caught in the base of her thumb and she could not release it. She had to paddle the canoe back to land with the fish stuck there. Mary Ann did the necessary surgery to remove the spike and treat the wound.

There were considerable dangers in the water. The electric eels, as their name suggested, could give a powerful electric shock, and used this both in hunting and in self defence. Sting rays were a hazard too. If anyone was unfortunate enough to stand on one in the water, the resulting injury was extremely painful, especially if the barb from the sting broke off in the wound. These injuries often became infected. If Shirley was there and had adequate supplies of antibiotics the treatment was usually successful, but if there was no proper treatment, recovery could be long and painful. The sting rays were more likely to lurk around the edge of the lake which explained why the adults tended to take a canoe even a few yards to the raft house when they went for a bath. Although the children splashed at the water's edge they probably churned up the water enough to discourage the sting rays.

Other dangers lurked in the water. The anaconda, which is the common name for the South American water snake, was not a frequent visitor but its presence was not completely unknown and it was to be feared. At 30 feet or more it is one of the largest and most powerful water snakes in the world. It is cleverly camouflaged and hides in the murky waters looking for food. It kills its prey by constricting it until bones are broken and suffocation occurs, whereupon it unhinges its jaws and swallows the meal whole. It is certainly a creature to be reckoned with.

Attacks from an anaconda were rare, but memorable when they did happen. On one occasion a father was out in a canoe with his young son, fishing together. Suddenly, without warning, an anaconda struck, appearing over the edge of the canoe and grabbing the man's upper leg. The boat rocked violently as the man put up a struggle. Fortunately, he had a machete to hand and fought off the huge creature. Had it been his small son, the outcome was likely to have been tragic. As he returned to the shore the bite was clearly visible around his thigh, and he himself was pulling snake teeth from the wound. He was badly shocked, realising just how fortunate his escape had been. Shirley patched him up as best she could.

There were other water snakes which were poisonous and land snakes too, which could also swim. The Paumarí did not eat snake meat. Piranha and alligators were also seen. It was a little surprising to discover that the Paumarí were very afraid of the porpoises which came up close from time to time. If their children were swimming at the time, they would immediately be called out of the water. They had been told by local people that there was a city at the bottom of the lake where the porpoises would take people.

There were several different kinds of turtle in the jungle and the Paumarí had different words for the male and females. The land turtle was a tortoise while one of the other species could almost have come from a textbook of prehistoric creatures. Watching the villagers kill a turtle required a strong stomach. The creatures seemed to have an uncanny sense of direction so the villagers would tie their front and back legs together to prevent escape. Whilst others in the local population killed them with a quick decapitation, the Paumarí felt that there was a more humane method. They would get a small stick and sharpen the end to something like a knitting needle. Then they would swiftly force it up the nose of the turtle until it pierced the brain.

Once the poor creature was dead by whichever debatable method had been used, they then cut the skin from the turtle shell around the front and back legs and neck with a sharp knife. An axe was then used to sever the top from the bottom of the shell. It was hard work. They themselves would eat the meat, offal, skin and fat. The shells were used either as cooking pots, or for bailing out canoes. Nothing was wasted. Turtle meat was delicious. It was always a treat to be offered some.

As the river water receded, the Paumarí were quick to plant along the beach. The ground here was very fertile due to the silt which came in the water. A crop of manioc or melons for example, could come to full maturity in six months in the rich soil, whereas higher up in the jungle, it might take up to two years. In high water the lake looked the colour of milky tea as it was heavily laden with silt. In low water it was nearly black due to the rotting vegetation. It was this water which Shirley and Mary Ann filtered and boiled, before using it as their drinking water. It was the same water which people used to bath and swim in. But there was no choice, although later on they acquired a water tank and were able to catch rain water off the roof.

Word had gone around that Shirley pulled teeth and before too long she had her first dental patient. She was so grateful for her lunchtime training back at the *Mildmay Hospital* but was as nervous, if not more so, than the patient sitting before her. She had a few instruments with her, but all of her limited experience had been on people who had received a whiff of anaesthetic. She did have some local anaesthetic and a book which a travelling dentist had given her on a little boat out of Manaus. Now, with her first patient ready and waiting, and with Mary Ann holding his head to stop him falling over backwards, Shirley took a quick dash into the bedroom, looked at the picture in the book which she had left open to remind herself where to put the injection, and then went back out to her patient with all the confidence she could muster!

Many people came for dental extractions and on one particularly busy Saturday she pulled one hundred teeth. It was exhausting work. Often the patient arrived complaining of toothache only for her to find a mouth devoid of any teeth. Hidden below the gum line were rotting roots. These were even more difficult to extract and the work often had to be done over several weeks. Even some of the small children had teeth worn down to the gum line. The mothers eventually explained that they had allowed the children to chew on unripe bananas and the acid had destroyed the enamel. One of their best language helpers needed to have her upper front teeth removed, but they discovered a surprise benefit from the lady's loss. Without her teeth they could distinguish between two different types of 'r' so much more easily!

For a short time Shirley also had some white material for temporary fillings. One elderly shaman - witch doctor - had a single tooth at the front and he came to ask for help. He did not want to have it extracted but it was very thin at the gum line. Shirley carefully built up the tooth with her white amalgam and for an amazingly long time the white filling gleamed from his otherwise toothless smile.

After a few months, Shirley and Mary Ann asked some of the men if they would add an extension to their house. Now that they had a means of paying for any work which was done for them, it was acceptable for them to make this request. Even with the best will in the world it was impossible to cook, live, eat, sleep, run a clinic, dental surgery, school and office for linguistic study in an area just ten feet square. They carefully drew up some plans.

Shirley smiled to herself from time to time as she remembered back to when she had thought that her nursing skills would be completely wasted. In one sense, she certainly was no longer a nurse in the traditional sense of tending patients according to the instructions given by a doctor. She was called on more and more to treat the sick in ways that only a doctor would do in a more developed environment. But when it was a matter of life and death, then it was worth having a go. She was so grateful that in addition to her own training, the power of God was clearly at work.

Shirley needed more and more local anaesthetic. It was not just for dentistry, but also for the first aid which she did to treat knife wounds and to remove splinters, thorns and fish hooks which had become embedded in a patient's skin. She ordered this in boxes of 500, and was amused to find that they came in parcels addressed to Dr S Chapman.

One day she was called to go to another village to see a man who was very sick. He seemed to be in the final stages of chronic heart failure. Shirley had no means of confirming her suspicions, but he was very swollen and short of breath. She had a few sample tablets on her and stressed to him that he should go downriver and get further help, although she did not really expect him to live long enough to do that. She made a note of his name and condition and left him with a prayer on his behalf. It was some long time later that she came across a man with the same name. Was it him? Indeed it was! She asked him what had happened.

"Oh, I got better with the tablets you gave me," he told her. Shirley knew that humanly speaking there was no way it could have happened. God had intervened.

On one occasion a lady was brought to her who had suffered an horrific accident in a boat. It had an inboard motor and as the lady had leant over the motor her long hair had got caught in the mechanism. She had been totally scalped. It was several days since the accident and the open wound was covered with what looked like brown paper. Shirley hardly knew where to start and even before she touched the dressing, the stench hit her. She quickly excused herself and took a gulp of air to try and control her own nausea. The wound was a total mass of pus.

She cleaned it up as best she could and gave the woman huge doses of antibiotics. She told the family members that they must take the lady downriver to the nearest town of Lábrea to try to get some expert help. This was a long journey, often taking twelve hours by canoe with outboard motor, and at that time it was just a small community with no hospital. She quickly wrote a letter to the mayor of the town, asking for his help. Perhaps from Lábrea they could get the lady to Manaus. Shirley often wondered what happened to the lady, and once again, did not expect her to survive. But survive she did – by the grace of God.

It was not always humans who needed urgent treatment. A dog was brought to Shirley one day having been in a fight with a wild animal. It had a slash wound from jaw to shoulder. It was a fairly ferocious animal and there was no way that Shirley was going to be able to touch it without it having had a general anaesthetic. She remembered that she had some ether. The tins of flour and other dried food often got contaminated with weevils, but a small amount of ether on a cotton wool ball stored in the tin, was very effective. How could she administer ether to her canine patient, she wondered? In the end she improvised by taking a tin and removing both ends. It served quite well as an anaesthetic mask, and she was able to stitch up the animal before it awoke.

As life continued to settle into some sort of routine, Shirley and Mary Ann came and went. They learnt to identify the sound of the Norseman as it came to collect them long before they could see it, and trips out to civilisation were always welcome. But the Paumarí were becoming friends, and it was strange to leave them. They doubted at first if the villagers trusted them to come back, but the Paumarí were slowly beginning to accept that these ladies were with them for the long haul. There was a growing and mutual respect and trust.

A difficult diagnosis

The rash was mysterious and she could not identify its cause. The fever left her exhausted and the cough hacked through her chest and throat. It was Shirley herself who was ill, and she had no idea what the problem was. She was concerned that she might have something infectious, and tried to stay as far away from people as possible, but in the village that was easier said than done. After feeling wretched for almost two weeks, she was more than ready to step into the float plane and be taken back to Manaus.

The doctor did some blood tests and found her white cell count to be extremely high. To her shock and horror, he suspected that she might have leukaemia. Further tests, however, revealed that she was actually suffering from a severe infestation of hookworm which had caused anaemia and which, in turn, had given an abnormally high white count. The diagnosis was a huge relief but the treatment was, nevertheless, very slow and she continued to feel unwell for some long time.

It had been several years now since Shirley had left England and she was due for home leave. This was expected to be for a year or more and she thought of it with mixed feelings. It would be so good to see family and friends again and to talk to her supporters and inspire them with the work that she was doing. But it was such a long time to leave the village and the prospect was daunting. Would she remember anything of what she had learnt, she wondered? What would happen to the precious relationships which she was building with these people?

She had a real longing in her heart that the Paumarí should have something of the scriptures in their own language before she left the following year. On one of their trips out, she and Mary Ann had talks with their director and discussed the possibilities. Mary Ann had already made a start at translating the creation story. Shirley had started with the gospel of Mark. They picked out what seemed at first sight to be simple stories, but then realised just how un-simple they really were. As Shirley worked on the story of the transfiguration with a language helper, they considered that the clothes Jesus was wearing were glistening and intensely white.[8]

The first suggestion from the Paumarí was to have a washer-woman bleaching them on the mountain! Even the word mountain was a problem as there was not a hill in sight.

Reflections on early days

Shirley thought about the huge changes which affected the community during the cycle of nature. The level of the water rose and fell by approximately 40 feet during the year. Daily life took a huge amount of time. There was their little garden to tend in order to supplement their diet. There were constant interruptions and always, always, people present.

[8] *And His garments became glistening, intensely white, as no fuller (cloth dresser, launderer) on earth could bleach them. Mark 9:3 (Amplified Bible)*

When the water was low enough Shirley took to walking in the jungle in the early afternoons, just to have some time to be alone. Medicine, dentistry, midwifery, linguistics and daily life made the days full to bursting.

Buster continued to provide entertainment. He did not like to get wet. Shirley and Mary Ann needed to get away for a while and as the water was high they took a canoe to paddle their way through the jungle for a visit to two colleagues who were working in another village on another language. Buster came too. But soon after they left the rains began and with it, they began to feel a little chilly. Buster was cold too so he climbed onto Shirley's lap and they huddled together for mutual warmth. But at one point Shirley and Mary Ann had to wade through a stream where they could not paddle the canoe, but they could not possibly carry Buster as well. He was forced to swim, and he was not a happy doggy. Back in the canoe he shivered and his look said it all. The canoe passed through some fairly thick foliage which was growing on the surface of the water. Buster, already looking for a way out, thought it was safe dry land, and took a flying leap. When they finally hauled him out, dripping wet again and covered with green slime, he was even more miserable and then, when they finally reached their destination and started to walk through the forest to the village, it was wet, muddy and slippery. Buster was not impressed.

Shirley dare not add his considerable weight to the float plane on their trips out of the village so Buster had to be left behind, often in the care of the local chief. He then had to scavenge like the other dogs and often used to look a little worse for wear when his ladies returned, although his robust health generally returned quite quickly. Rosa, however, was more fragile. On their return to the village from the first trip out to Manaus, they discovered that Rosa had pined for them so much and had refused to eat. She had starved herself to death.

8 Home (and back)

The sound of the baby's crying had gone on for what seemed like hours, and in the end Shirley could bear it no longer. She simply had to go and find out what was causing the little one such distress. She followed the sound of the noise which got louder as she approached the house, but to her surprise, no one seemed to be around. Surely they had not left a baby alone in the house? She called out to the owners, but there was no response. It was some moments before she caught sight of the parrot and then her concern turned to laughter. The parrot had been doing an excellent mimic of a crying baby and she had been totally taken in! It was clear that in jungle life it was not always the humans who had the last laugh.

As she continued her plans for home leave to England, the Paumarí were anxious.

"How long will you be away?" one asked.

"Are you going to come back?" another questioned nervously. "We will all die when you are away."

As she explained to them the number of times the waters would come and go while she was away, eighteen months certainly did sound a very long time. She assured them that she would come back, but as for their other concerns, she knew that in reality some of them would probably die without medical help.

She tried to explain her journey to England and who she would see when she was there, but it was almost impossible to convey the idea of continents and oceans to people who had never been further than their village. As she thought of the comparisons between life in England and survival in the jungle, there was a stark contrast. Although she had lived through a war, she had never gone hungry to the degree that these people faced hunger. She had always had a choice of what to wear. If people were ill they made an appointment to see their doctor and got sent to hospital if necessary. If they were really sick then a phone call would bring an ambulance.

The children went to school where there were teachers, books and endless other resources. They even received one third of a pint of milk each day, free. She often wondered what that quantity of milk would do for the health of these little ones with whom she lived. For the Paumarí, life was a constant challenge for survival. She could offer them treatment for intestinal worms, only to watch them swallow it down with worm infested water from the lake. Their diet was limited and very often there was simply not enough food. In high water it was particularly hard to catch fish as they were spread over such a vast area.

But on the other hand, she needed to go back and see her family and supporters. She must touch base with her own roots for a while. She could not expect the Paumarí to understand just how important it was for her to update her supporters and to inspire them with what she was doing. All the gifts which were given to her were channelled through Wycliffe. There was no other source of income or salary. These gifts had to cover every aspect of her life and work. Food and clothing, housing, flights and other travel, equipment, medicines, payment of language helpers, publication of literacy and translation materials, all had to come from the gifts of her supporters.

Each member had to produce an annual budget. It was partly based on their country of work but other factors included their location and type of ministry. Someone working, for example, in an office in town, would have less financial demands than those in a village location. Any gifts which were sent to Wycliffe but not designated for one particular person or project were put into an emergency fund. Shirley often found that she qualified to receive extra support from this fund. She never liked doing it and its resources were limited, but the cost of helping so many people in need was considerable. Although some medicine was provided through the government, the rest was bought by Shirley, but it was often impossible to make ends meet without this extra help.

She tried to remind the Paumarí that they had seen her come and go for a while now. When she left the village to go back to Manaus to study and replenish supplies, had she not always come back? It was just that this time she would be away for longer. It was with mixed feelings that she had heard that she would be expected to teach at the SIL language course for three months during two consecutive summers, and it was with equally mixed feelings that she was going at all. She was committed to these people and was growing to love them. Where was home and who was family?

Her flight was booked for early May (1966) and in the meantime, life alternated between routine and drama. A small child was badly scalded when a pot of coffee fell over, and its tiny chest and abdomen were severely blistered.

The days were so busy but there were always interruptions in the village. People wanting medical help, people wanting this, people wanting that... people, always people. It was so hard to concentrate. The tasks seemed overwhelming and the weeks were never long enough.

At times Shirley would even resort to hiding in the jungle for some solitude. On one occasion a Paumarí family hid her inside the mosquito net where their daughter was in isolation prior to the puberty festival. Unfortunately, the family who were looking for her decided to sit and wait for her in the same house, so she and the young girl had to sit in total silence! Eventually the visitors tired of waiting.

Within SIL, plans were in hand to build a centre on the outskirts of the small town of Porto Velho. This was welcomed with great enthusiasm as there had never been an official centre in Manaus. When the village workers went out with the pilot, they often stayed in his own home or with any other willing host. This often meant that children were turned out of their bedrooms and Shirley, among others, were never completely comfortable in doing so. People were so generous but they had limited space.

A centre in Porto Velho would have many advantages. For a start, it would only involve a flight of about one hour instead of four or five and that would be of great benefit in terms of time, energy and fuel for which each member paid when needing the plane. If necessary, Shirley could bring out really sick patients for some more specialised treatment, to say nothing of lessening her own travel sickness.

Suitable land had been found a few miles out of town which had reasonable access to both the river and the airport. It meant that the float plane could be used there immediately the centre was up and running, and that in the future when they hoped to have wheel planes, a runway was nearby.

Teams continued to live in town until work began. Gradually about 25 private homes were built. There were plans too for a radio shop, school buildings, study centre and office. Houses would be built at a great enough distance to give some privacy, but not too far to visit a neighbour. It would be a real home from home for SIL teams, and a place of refuge from the pressures of village life. The members' children would have some formal schooling while the family was on the centre, and the adults could consolidate their work so far and have time to reflect and study without endless interruptions. It would be a suitable and safe place to bring out language helpers for workshops. Building progress was followed with eager expectation.

The Summer Institute of Linguistics had an agreement with the National Museum of Brazil, and later on with the University of Brasilia, that any material they produced should be archived with them. The National Museum had been established back in 1818 to record scientific interest, natural history, ethnology and anthropology. When it was decided just how the Paumarí alphabet would be presented, this also had to be submitted to the National Museum for approval. The centre at Porto Velho provided an excellent base for such communications.

Back in the village, a family moved in with Shirley and Mary Ann. The mother – whom they called Jumper – had given birth to ten children but only two girls, named Gisi and Fátima, had survived. Jumper was a widow and had no one to build a house for her. She was more than happy to look after the house while they were away.

The day came when it was time to say goodbye to these people who were becoming more than just neighbours. She could indeed class many of them as friends. The Paumarí were not noted for emotion and the idea of giving a hug as a farewell gesture was definitely not part of their culture. Hand shaking was not known to them either, and neither was waving. Indeed, on occasions when Shirley waved to someone as an instinctive reaction, they had stared firstly at her and then at her hand in the air with a look of total bewilderment.

Time had become quite short so there was just the briefest stop in Manaus before Shirley caught a connection to Rio and her international flight to London. Mary Ann was returning to the States for her home leave. There had been little time for adequate communication with home and Shirley was aware that her father would not know where to meet her, only that she was coming by air and not by ship.

As she stepped through the doors of the Arrivals area at Gatwick airport, the noise and the bustle seemed so strange. Although she was so used to people, this was very different. She felt like an alien. Just then she heard an announcement over the Tannoy system.

"Would Shirley Chapman, recently arrived from Rio de Janeiro, please come to the Information Desk."

She edged her trolley through the crowds and found the desk where a message was waiting from her father. He said that he had not known whether she would arrive at London's Heathrow airport or Gatwick, but if she phoned him he would come and meet her. She realised that it would take him several hours to drive across London, so she phoned him from the desk and told him that she would make her own way on the underground system, and they could meet at the local station.

It was a bit of an anticlimax to arrive back and not have someone there to meet her. She sorted out a ticket and reminded herself of which way she would need to go. Even by train it would take more than an hour and a half, and she was grateful for a seat as she settled back into the carriage as it rattled its way under the streets of London. It felt like a different world from the village and she wondered just how much of her study into the language she would actually remember by the time she got back.

The London accent seemed so strange to her now, and yet she had grown up speaking it. She tried not to stare, but some of the young people had the most amazing hair. They had shaved the side parts and had the top styled into dramatic spikes. As for the colour... bright reds and green! She had never seen anything like it. She felt surprisingly cold, and wished that she had a coat. She had been wearing one when she left England as it had been chilly then too, and had put it into a cleaners in Rio. It was so beautifully wrapped in plastic when she collected it, and there it had stayed for the whole time she had been away. As she had made her plans for home leave, she got the coat out of the bag, only to find that it was totally mouldy and beyond hope. Moisture must have got in somehow and the coat was ruined.

The central line train emerged above ground and she realised they were nearly there. Tiredness and emotion were catching up as a lump caught in her throat at the thought of seeing her father again. As she hauled her luggage through the station, suddenly there he was!

It was strange to be sleeping in her old room once more. She knew that she had changed in five years and that he probably had too. They would have to adjust to living together again. Sydney still smoked heavily and she noted that the dining room ceiling was stained and greasy from years of cigarette smoke. She wondered what it was doing to his fragile lungs, already weakened by years of TB. His cough spoke volumes. The fumes were a bit claustrophobic and at times the solid walls of the house closed in on her after her flimsy house in the village and the open air of the jungle. It was, however, good to see him and she looked forward to meeting up with many of her old friends too.

After breakfast together the next morning, her father took her into the town to buy a coat. Her next stop was to visit the doctor. She knew that she was still not well. The doctor felt that she should be seen by specialists in tropical medicine, and gave her a letter of referral. It was not long before she had an appointment at the *Hospital for Tropical Diseases* in London, and only a few days later she was admitted there for further investigations. She spent a week in hospital while they did further tests on the hookworm problem, and gave some expert treatment.

After that early drama of being home, it was good when life began to settle down into some sort of routine, and she could begin to catch up properly with family, friends and supporters.

One of the highlights of the time in England was to receive some letters from the Paumarí. They were a little unorthodox in presentation, but Shirley was excited to see the progress they were making in her absence. They had clearly been practicing and that was so encouraging.

The Paumarí reported on the death of three small babies. It was sad news and Shirley wondered whether she might have been able to give them a chance if she had been there. It was impossible to tell. However, the rest of the village sounded in reasonably good health and that was excellent. Their house had some occupants. Rats and mice had taken up residence and along with the usual insects, had done a huge amount of damage. The roof was leaking badly. Clearly it would need some extensive repairs or even a rebuild when they got back.

It was during that first home leave that she was on holiday with a friend, and it involved a long journey back to London. June, who was driving, had only recently passed her test and was anxious about the responsibility. Some of the people whom they had met during their time away gathered around them to pray for June to cope with the challenge of a long drive. They prayed too that Shirley would not be travel sick. Much later on she realised with some astonishment that she had not suffered from travel sickness since then. In fact, God had done more than had been asked and had dealt with the problem completely.

As Shirley shared about her work, one of the questions which came up from time to time was on the terminology of the word Indian. Why, some people asked, were the Paumarí called Indians when they had never been anywhere near India and lived in Brazil? It was an interesting question.

From the best of her own understanding, Shirley explained that way back South America had been occupied by lots of ethnic groups, each with their own language and culture. In the 1500-1600s groups of people came from Europe all seeking land. They thought that they had arrived in India and thus called the people Indians. Different groups from Portugal, Spain and Holland all fought over South America, and Brazil eventually became a territory of Portugal and adopted its language. Most of the rest of South America came under Spanish jurisdiction.

As a result of these invasions, the indigenous groups were pushed back further and further into isolated land. It often sounded as though there was a distinction between the Paumarí and Brazilians, although they had in fact all been born in Brazil. However, deep suspicions remained between them with disputes over land and rights. The term 'Indian' was slowly being brought into question. The Paumarí greatly disliked the Portuguese word 'Indian' being applied to them as it conveyed the idea of a naked cannibal.

The weeks and months sped past. Her father's health concerned her and Shirley made a secret visit to his doctor to see if she could find out any more about his current health status.

"I really do not know how he is still alive," the doctor replied thoughtfully. "I cannot give you any definite prognosis."

A question began to go round and round in Shirley's mind. Should she leave him and go back to Brazil? Or should she stay until he had died. She felt very unsettled and unsure of what was the right thing to do. In the end she felt that she had to make some sort of decision. She would make plans to return unless the Lord showed her very clearly that she should do otherwise. Very shortly after that her father expressed his own opinion.

"I do not want you staying around waiting for me to die. I want you to go back."

A neighbour also said something similar. "You know, your father does not want you to wait around for him to die. He wants you to go back."

The return journey to Brazil (October 1967) was to be made by ship, although on a slightly less impressive vessel than her first voyage. When she had stood on the deck of the *SS United States* on the first occasion and waved to her father, she had sensed that she would see him again. This time there were no such feelings. It felt to her that this goodbye might be final.

She was grateful to the friends who were sensitive to this real possibility, and who prayed discreetly for her and Sydney.

The *SS Amazon* left Tilbury Docks and as it headed down the River Thames towards the North Sea, there were several places along the Essex coast which were familiar. This time round there were no friends on board to share the journey and Shirley found that she was to share a cabin with a stranger. The young Brazilian lady, however, was also a Christian, so they were both delighted, and the process of getting acquainted helped with the emotion of watching the coast of England disappear into the distance.

The lady had been studying church music in England for a year and Shirley subsequently stayed with her family in Rio as part of the open invitation she had from them. Another lady on the ship had been in England for nine months, during which time she had lived with a Brazilian couple. She had barely managed to learn any English at all, and had become a virtual prisoner in their house. Shirley was able to befriend her during the 5000 mile journey and to talk to her in Portuguese. She also gave the lady a Portuguese New Testament which she read avidly, and which clearly had a profound effect on her.

The boat sailed into the harbour at Rio on an overcast morning with the view of the beautiful city totally obscured by cloud. It was good to be back on Brazilian soil. The passage through Customs was relatively straightforward, which was a huge relief. It also looked as though she might get a free flight to Brasilia and also on to Porto Velho. The Brazilian Air Force seemed quite happy to take passengers if they had spare room in their planes and were also willing to carry them free.

While Shirley had been away, there had been some changes in the law relating to some of the smaller aircraft. Tighter restrictions were needed to combat drug and contraband problems. It meant, however, that some of JAARS planes were grounded. Mission surveys had come to a halt and travel for teams to their villages would be much more complicated. It was hard to see how the problem might be resolved.

Another problem causing concern was to do with visas. Once again, there had been a change in the law, this time regarding permanent visas and, as a result, Mary Ann was delayed in the States. It was not encouraged for workers to go to village situations alone, and Shirley wondered just how these two issues would be resolved.

As she waited in town for news of Mary Ann's arrival, a number of emergencies demanded her attention. One morning the radio man came looking for her. He reported that another team urgently required a box of penicillin to help in a measles epidemic. They dashed into town and bought the antibiotics and then raced to the airport. It would still take the best part of a week for the medication to reach the village, but they were distressed to find that the flight had left early and they had missed it.

There was nothing else which could be done that day, and the following morning another emergency arose. A lady had been taking high doses of steroids for asthma, but had run out of supplies. Shirley went back into town, purchased the medication and hurried to the airport where the pilot was waiting. She went on the flight with him so as to be available to help the lady if required, and they were able to deliver both lots of medication. The measles patients were spared the wait and some lives were possibly saved.

There was no news of Mary Ann's visa. Another couple were due to travel back to their village, so Shirley went with them. They informed her that there were about one hundred teeth waiting to be pulled. During the three weeks she spent with them, dentistry took up much of the time. Mary Ann was finally able to get her documents in order, and once she had arrived back in Brazil, she and Shirley went back to the Paumarí together.

The contents of the house had not been tampered with, but the structure itself was in a sorry state. Termites had taken up residence in the roof. A swarm of angry hornets were not happy about being evicted and the ensuing battle was not without casualties on both sides. Cockroaches were everywhere. Mould and rust had taken its toll. There was much spring cleaning to be done. Nevertheless, it was good to be back.

It took three weeks of hard work to get the house shipshape and that included having a new roof. The old one was beyond repair. They arranged for a little structure to be built a short distance into the jungle, and the improvised screened office provided a welcome sanctuary from people. It was good both for study and for personal reflection.

Once more the radio brought news of a problem. The village teams were able to talk to each other and Shirley had often become the medic of the airways. A couple reported that their young son was unwell and the tips of his fingers had become white and were then gradually turning black. Shirley's heart sank. She had seen a similar case back at *Mildmay* where a young girl had been taken repeatedly to theatre for amputation, firstly of her fingers and then limbs. It had been most distressing.

For the family who were now caught up in a similar crisis, a chain of miraculous events began to unfold. Shirley advised them to get the boy out for expert medical help as soon as possible, and initially the mother took him on an emergency flight to Porto Velho. However, the doctor was so concerned and advised that he be taken to Rio or São Paulo immediately. The father needed to join them and made hasty arrangements. The diagnosis on the boy was arteritis, a disease which was attacking the arteries in his body and which could indeed result in amputation. It was felt that if they could stop it from attacking his vital organs, his life could be spared. They were advised to return to the States without delay. Throughout these anxious days, one thing after another and then another 'just happened'. Not only were flights available where and when they needed them, but doctors were in the right place at the right time.

The boy knew enough to realise that he might lose some fingers and he was distraught. He was so distressed that surgery to amputate had to be delayed. But then an amazing thing started to happen. His circulation began to return and the gangrene slowly disappeared! Surgery was no longer needed. The boy was restored.

Alongside encouragements there were also disappointments. Some of the young girls were impatient for a husband and there were also some young widows who wanted a new man. There had been a fair amount of immorality with some non-indigenous men in the area but affection seemed a little lacking. These men did not want to live in the village and the girls did not want to go with the men. However, two of the girls were pregnant but it was unclear as to who would take care of them and what their future might hold. But it was difficult to remain single in either culture. There were reports of some abortions.

Some of the personal stories which emerged were indeed sad and complex. It was a struggle to understand their personal stories through the language barrier, and to know how to respond with wisdom and compassion. Oh for the day when they would have the word of God to help them.

Gisi had married a Brazilian river trader. She and her sister Fátima, together with their mother Jumper, were no longer living with Shirley and Mary Ann, although they were all valuable language helpers. Gisi's first baby was big and the labour was difficult. Despite Shirley's protests, the men tried to push it out and the baby was stillborn.

Shirley longed to introduce God to them and yet the challenge seemed almost insurmountable. How could she, with their limited mutual language, explain an awesome yet invisible being? She remembered Moses asking God a similar question.[9] She thought of the many 'I am's' associated with the answer God gave him, and longed for the Paumarí to experience the reality of knowing Jesus as "I am the light of the world..."[10] to show them the way. "I am the bread of life..."[11] to feed them physically and spiritually. "I am the good shepherd..."[12] to lead them, protect them and provide for them. But whilst she had worked out the word for lamp light, moon light, sun light, day light...how should she describe the light of the world? How could she explain what a shepherd was? Somehow the 'farinha of life' did not have quite the same ring to it as bread. In any case, she would need to explain bread, where it came from and so on.

The more she thought, the more questions tumbled over themselves in her brain. How could she describe to them who Jesus was? Yes – they might relate to the fact that someone lived in similar circumstances to their own, but the concept that Jesus was the Son of God, that He died but was brought back to life... where and how should she start? How could she explain the circumstances and reason for His coming, and the awesome message of His death? How could she explain salvation until she found a suitable word? How could she expound the Trinity? How could she tell them that the Holy Spirit was indeed a person, although one they could

[9] *And Moses said to God, Behold, when I come to the Israelites and say to them, The God of your fathers has sent me to you, and they say to me, What is His name? What shall I say to them?*

And God said to Moses, I AM WHO I AM and WHAT I AM, and I WILL BE WHAT I WILL BE; and He said, You shall say this to the Israelites, I AM has sent me to you. Exodus 3:13-14 (Amplified Bible)

[10] *Thoughts from John 8:12*

[11] *Thoughts from John 6:35*

[12] *Thoughts from Psalm 23*

not see, who could give them power to live their lives with purpose and dignity? The longer her list of questions grew, the more impossible it seemed.

There were no easy answers and yet, in quiet ways, the lives of Shirley and Mary Ann began to demonstrate the truths they hoped to share. In asking the question of how the Paumarí could understand what it was to trust in God, Shirley began to realise that the people were beginning to trust her and Mary Ann in ways they did not trust each other. They began to leave their valuables with them when they went on a journey, but they would not do that with each other. God, in His own inimitable way was beginning to show some of the answers.

Some of the Paumarí were very keen to act as language helpers, first in the analysis and later in translation, especially as they would be paid for their work. They loved to recount stories onto a tape recorder of their trips out fishing or hunting. These were then transcribed with the help of the author, and later analysed.

As they assisted in translating the word of God, slowly but surely the truth of what they were reading began to affect their lives. One Paumarí lady was deeply affected by the story of Herod being challenged by John the Baptist about having taken his brother's wife for himself.[13] She herself had left her husband and married his brother. God's word had spoken to her more clearly than anyone could have done and she realised that she was totally in the wrong.

Another lady helped with the translation of the story of Zaccheaus.[14] As a tax collector he had been hated as it was common in the trade for them to exploit people by demanding extra taxes and keeping the change. This lady had stolen a duck, but now was so convicted that she took

[13] *From Mark 6:18 – no specific translation*
[14] *From Luke 19:8 – no specific translation*

back the duck with four ducklings. How true it is that the word of God is alive and active.

One day Chico came rushing into the house. He asked how he could get his pet parrot down. Normally it would be kept on a piece of vine, but on this occasion he had used some plastic cord. The parrot had somehow managed to get free and now it was sitting at the top of a very tall tree with the plastic cord twisted around the branch.

The tree was covered in thorns and there was no way that anyone would be able to climb high enough to catch the parrot. It was a bit drastic to chop the tree down in order to reclaim the parrot, and he reasoned, with some justification, that the parrot would probably die in the process. Shirley did not have any helpful suggestions to offer.

Some time later she heard the sound of an axe against a tree. The noise went on for hours and she guessed that Chico had decided to cut the tree down after all. Eventually there came the sound of crashing. Moments later Chico came rushing into the house.

"Your God is powerful!" he exclaimed breathlessly. Shirley looked surprised and realised that she had not even thought to bring God into the problem.

"I asked Him to look after my parrot," Chico explained. "And He did! When the tree fell down all the branches were broken except the one on which the parrot had been sitting. That was sticking up in the air and my parrot was fine. God is great!" Who could argue with that?

As translation work continued, the language helpers were generally enthusiastic and reasonably reliable in their work, and initial checks progressed on several different books. Questions were nearly always thought provoking.

Shirley remembered Babadi, and him sitting expectantly, waiting for the next question in a translation workshop. They were thinking about Jairus and the death of his daughter.[15] Jesus had asked:

"Why are you crying? The child is not dead, she is only sleeping."

"Babadi," Shirley turned to look at him. "Was Jairus' daughter dead?"

"No. She was asleep," Babadi replied without hesitation.

"How do you know she was asleep?"

"Because Jesus said so and Jesus does not lie," Babadi replied confidently.

It took them a while to get the child dead in their translation so that she could be raised to life!

Jumper proved to be an excellent language helper, improvising explanations which assisted everyone to work their way through some of these discussions. But there was still a shortage of suitable Paumarí words for some basic truths. God... Saviour... sin... grace... forgiveness... sacrifice... these were just a few of them.

One lady decided most definitely that she was going to be a language helper. She wanted to buy a new case and here was a way to earn some money. In many ways she was not a good teacher, but in another sense, she was invaluable. In the Paumarí language there were two different 'r' sounds. These were used in 50-60% of words but it was extremely difficult to distinguish the difference, and neither was like the 'r' in English. It needed a real knack to curl the tongue in order the get the right sound. The fish lady, as she somehow got named, was excellent in this respect. She refused to let Shirley get away with anything less that the right sound, and her tough approach finally paid off.

The old Norseman was now out of service and the SIL members were waiting for a new float plane to arrive from the States. When the first attack of malaria struck, Shirley was

---

[15] From Mark 5: 22-23 and 35-43 – no specific translation

in Porto Velho, and was laid low. She desperately needed some time out but would not have chosen to be sick. The centre was not yet completed and she was living in makeshift lodgings at the end of the school room. It was not ideal, but better than nothing. She and Mary Ann had brought their cat with them and Puddy decided to come and share her bed, snuggling down cosily by her feet. As Shirley dozed fitfully, she wondered at first if she was dreaming. She was not. The cat had just delivered four kittens in the bed!

For a while there was no other option but to rest. She was reminded of the words in Isaiah. "For thus said the Lord God, the Holy One of Israel: In returning (to Me) and resting (in Me) you shall be saved: in quietness and in (trusting confidence) shall be your strength. But you would not, And you said 'No! We will speed on...'" [16]

[16] *Isaiah 30: 15-16a (Amplified Bible)*

Shirley with Buster
(and Rosa on the roof)

9 News

It was nearly Christmas (1969) and this year they would not be in the village, but spending it with colleagues at the new centre in Porto Velho. Shirley had become midwife there, and one of the members had a baby due. The centre was proving to be a real oasis. Shirley and Mary Ann shared a house with two other single ladies. They had a rota system when they were all together in order to share the cooking and other chores. It seemed as though Shirley often got called to act as nurse as well as midwife. She was grateful to Mary Ann who would willingly cover her rotas in the house when she got called away.

During Christmas week there was plenty of post and it was lovely to sit and read greetings from family and friends. One day, however, two telegrams arrived together with messages from England. She looked at the dates and opened the first one from her brother. It stated simply, "Dad very sick". She could guess the content of the second one even before she opened it. "Dad died." She sat for a while with the messages in her hand and memories of her father flooded over her. It was remarkable that his lungs had functioned for as long as they had.

For a while she went back in time to the day when she had sat in the neighbour's house waiting for news of her mother. Even now she felt the knot of grief which had formed in her stomach that day and the terrible feeling of emptiness and hopelessness when her father had come to tell her that she had died. What grief he himself had known. Now he was gone. It would be strange not to write to him and have his letters in return. Part of her longed to be back in England and attend his funeral, but it was an impossible time to leave. The telegrams had taken several days to arrive and it was already too late.

The expectant mother went into labour and it was good to have something definite to do. The baby seemed as though it might be on the large side and Shirley was just a little anxious at possible complications. In the event, baby Carolyn was born safely – at a healthy 10lb 8oz. She was the first baby to be born on the Porto Velho centre. As colleagues celebrated Christmas together, they rejoiced at the humble coming of Jesus as a tiny and helpless baby, of the new life safely delivered, and surrounded Shirley with love and understanding as she remembered Sydney.

Back in the village, the busyness of daily life and work continued. It was never particularly easy to hold classes in the evening as the light from a paraffin lamp was so poor and the blackboard was all but lost in the darkness. Shirley managed to acquire a generator and this was a cause of much interest. Their pilot rigged it up for them so that they could have light. That was a huge advantage but there was a down side. It made so much noise and now, although they could see, they could not hear!

Never ones to be beaten by a problem, they asked some of the men to build a small shack specifically for the generator, about thirty feet or so from the back door. It was on stilts like all the other houses and had split palm floors and walls, and a leafy roof. It looked very smart and when darkness fell they took the generator to its new home and started it up. Students could now see and hear. There was no excuse. As time passed some vines started to grow around the generator's shack. They produced some beautiful flowers and it did look pretty. Someone said that they were called Morning Glory.

One morning, some visitors from outside the village came by to ask for medical help. They caught sight of the generator house and immediately stopped. With the utmost reverence they approached the shack, making the sign of the cross and bowing before it. Shirley and Mary Ann were mesmerised. Their generator seemed to have become a 'saint'.

By now they had a two-way radio and made contact with Porto Velho most mornings. Their village saint had become well known on the centre, and when she was sick, they would start her up in time for the radio messages so that the wheezing noises from her chest could be diagnosed over the air. Suitable treatment was then offered or, if the matter was too serious, she would be taken away for intensive care. It was a sad day when news reached them that their saint had suffered a fatal heart attack and would no longer be returning to the village. It was only many, many years later that they discovered that Morning Glory was also known by another name – Our Lady's Mantle.

Everyday life was often interrupted by the unexpected, but this particular day had started like any other. As dawn broke over the jungle the villagers began their activities. Small children were playing outside their houses while some of the older ones were down by the edge of the lake. Some of the men were already out in their canoes trying to fish for their family's breakfast, while a varied host of animals scavenged for scraps of food around the base of the houses.

As Shirley went about her morning routine, she marvelled that for them, the morning was unusual. For once, they were alone! Without having to step around and socialise with various visitors, the chores were done in double quick time, and Shirley was ready and waiting to take the morning call on the radio.

The voice which came over the air in Portuguese was familiar, but it sounded strained. It was almost as though he was talking in a whisper.

"Shirley, is that you? Are you alone? I have some news for both of you and I want to give it just to you."

Her heart began to beat faster. She sensed this was bad news. She was able to reassure him that they were indeed alone, and looking back later she realised just how remarkable that was.

"Shirley," he said slowly and with a lowered voice. He spoke in English which surprised her. It was not the language of the air. "Shirley, I have some bad news. There has been a plane crash."

Shirley's hand was trembling as she took further details. As she switched off the radio at the end of the message she felt as though her strength had drained away. She was deeply shocked. She fought back tears as she considered the task before her.

Baby Adiné had been born with a brain hernia. This looked like a tumour between her eyes where the bridge of her nose should have been. She was a sweet and loveable little girl with a winning smile, but it was clear that she needed specialist surgical treatment. Shirley had decided, therefore, to take the baby and her mother Magaga with her to Porto Velho and seek the advice of doctors there.

It was important for Shirley to inform FUNAI that she was there with the mother and baby. FUNAI is the National Indian Foundation, the department of the Brazilian government which establishes and carries out policies relating to the indigenous peoples. Everyone was agreed that the baby needed specialist neuro-surgery and that she should be transferred to Brasilia for treatment. FUNAI gave all the necessary help in making the arrangements.

It was felt by FUNAI that it would be too costly and complicated to take the mother too, and that Magaga should return to the village. This decision came as a big shock to Shirley as she realised that she herself would be a surrogate mum to this little one for the foreseeable future.

The baby was still being breast-fed so in addition to all the changes in her little life, being apart from her mother and away from her familiar culture, she had to adapt to bottle feeds. Her condition had resulted in some deformity in the palette of her mouth and she found it difficult to suck on a hard teat. Shirley had to improvise as best she could and eventually they found a way to get milk into the little girl. But it was a challenge to care for her. Not surprisingly, Adiné was frightened and unsettled and, as a result, Shirley found that precious hours slipped past as she did her best to comfort and feed the fractious baby.

Adiné was admitted to hospital but one delay after another meant that days and then weeks slipped past. Shirley was concerned at the baby's general condition and in some desperation asked to take the baby out of hospital and back to the village for a few months until surgery could be re-scheduled. The hospital authorities finally agreed to this, on one condition. Shirley was to spend a week at the hospital learning how to care for a baby! However, if that was the only way to get the baby out, then she decided to swallow her pride and learn her lessons well. In the event, she found herself busy all week in the children's ward helping to feed several little ones.

Back in Porto Velho Shirley was concerned at Adiné's condition. This previously happy child was a shadow of her former self and cried so much, especially when anyone tried to change her nappy. Her legs were swathed in bandages from infected areas where drips had been put in and transfusions given, but even so, Shirley was concerned at the level of her pain. She then began to wonder if the baby had a broken leg and that did indeed prove to be the case. No one knew how it had happened but she had a fracture at the hip. It explained a lot of her distress.

Plans were made immediately by a paediatrician in Porto Velho for her to go to another hospital for surgery on her leg. Shirley had given much more time than she had anticipated in caring for the baby, and was needed back in the village to prepare for a linguistic workshop. Gisela Kruck, a German colleague, had been with Mary Ann on a temporary assignment while Shirley was away, and it was planned for Gisela to take over as companion to the baby to enable Shirley to go back to the village. So it was that the float plane which brought Shirley back into the village, took Gisela out on the return flight.

The baby's mother was naturally anxious to have updates on her daughter, and Shirley did her best to give as good a report as she could muster. Inwardly, she was desperately sad by the whole affair. Back in Porto Velho, Gisela and the baby had been given seats on a flight of the Brazilian Air Force, and made their way to the airport. The plane went first to Manaus where everyone spent the night.

The next morning, soon after take-off the pilot reported engine trouble and turned back. As he landed a tyre burst and the plane erupted in flames. A number of people did manage to escape the inferno, but sixteen people did not. Among those who perished were Gisela and baby Adiné.

So it was that Shirley sat staring at the now silent radio receiver. She herself could so easily have been lost on that plane. She had spent so many weeks with the baby and it was only at the last minute that plans changed for Gisela to take her place. She was close to tears but she had a job to do. She must go and tell Magaga that her baby would never be coming home. They wept together.

The whole village was badly shaken and saddened by the tragedy. There was not just the human element of the crash but in their belief system someone who was burned had absolutely no hope of going to the 'renewal land'. Burials were completed quickly in Brazil. Gisela and the baby were buried together in Manaus. There was no time for anyone from the village to go. Although Gisela had only been in the village for a short time, she was well loved by the Paumarí, and they grieved for her.

The Paumarí's feelings about death were just a small part of their belief system. Shirley and Mary Ann had realised for some time that a deeper understanding of this aspect of village life was an important part of living with them.

Animism was a large part of the culture, and as far as the Paumarí were concerned they believed that all animals, fish, birds and even trees had a spirit. They felt that there was a deer spirit, a jaguar spirit, fish and bird spirits and so on, with the spirit of the jaguar being the strongest.

In order to be able to eat the meat of the various animals, it was important for every person to have gone through the rituals to appease the spirit of that kind of creature. They had taboos over eating snake meat and iguana; also meat from birds which had eaten dead and rotting meat, but whether these particular ones were due to perceived spirits was never really clear.

As far as the Paumarí were concerned, once a person had gone through the right ritual, then they had protection for life and were permitted to eat that particular meat. It was almost like a vaccination to give life-long immunity.

When a certain animal was killed, the adults were able to eat the meat as they would have gone through the ritual when they were younger. But they would keep the bones of the animal in readiness for a night-time ritual with the shaman which would – in their understanding – protect their children. Every child, therefore, had to go through lots of rituals in order to get protection from all the different spirits of any edible kind of meat.

The rituals were always performed at night. The shaman and the other men of the village would sit in a row on logs. The women and babies squatted in a circle in front of them. Other villagers would sit around behind this inner circle. In the early years Shirley and Mary Ann attended the rituals, so that they could understand this aspect of Paumarí culture and better translate scripture in a meaningful way. They could pick up from the singing that there was a particular tune for each animal. It seemed as though the tune itself was more important than any special words, and the men and women would sing the tune back and forth to each other.

The shaman, and then the rest of the men, would then take bones of the relevant animal and stroke them carefully as though extracting something from them. They then went around the group of women, stroking the head of the babies, each man stroking each child. During this part of the ritual there had to be total quietness. They believed that the spirit of the shaman had departed and that if there was a sudden noise, the spirit of the animal would take fright and also leave the shaman and the men. In that state they believed the person would die.

There were also elaborate and lengthy rituals surrounding the puberty rites. When a young girl reached the age of initiation she was kept in a mat wigwam or a mosquito net. Preparations started days in advance. The women gathered a large pile of bananas and plantains. These were skinned to the sound of singing, and then made into mushy balls ready for cooking. It was a real honour that Shirley and Mary Ann were allowed into the proceedings as the Paumarí were normally very anxious to keep the festa as a private event. The banana mixture of cooked, ripe and unripe bananas served as food for the spirit controlling the shaman and was consumed during the ritual.

By scraping the jenipapo fruit they produced some dye and used this to paint the girls with elaborate designs. The men had caught some fish and turtles and these were food for everyone else. Dancing and eating went on for several days and nights. It was an exhausting business. The final part of the ceremony involved all the women going into the jungle to collect large leaves and make headdresses. The young girls sat on mats while the women danced around them, flapping wet leaves up and down. If it had been raining heavily then this became more of a hopping, sliding and slipping ceremony and usually ended up with lots of helpless laughter. This was followed by several more ceremonial games resembling our 'tug-of-war' and 'catch me if you can'. Perhaps one day they would understand what it all meant.

As in any other culture, beliefs and traditions were a large part of Paumarí life. A woman was required to stay in the house for two weeks after a baby was born, together with the baby. Perhaps more surprising was that her husband was not allowed to do heavy work such as cutting wood, harvesting rubber or carrying heavy loads. They could eat small fish, farinha, rice or eggs, and the husband was allowed to go and prepare these for his wife. In time it became clear that the tradition concerning only eating small fish did make sense. If the mother ate the larger, fatty fish, it could affect her milk and upset the baby's digestion. Other customs surrounding births were not quite so easily explained.

The Paumarí believed that illnesses could be sucked out of the patient and that certain people had the special skills to do this. They could be quite proficient at producing an object which they had apparently sucked out of the person. One lady who professed to have this special ability performed her sucking out on a small baby who had dysentery, and apparently produced a large winged seed from its body. She watched in triumph as the baby got better, completely ignoring the fact that Shirley had been giving it the appropriate medicine.

Shirley questioned their sucking theories and caused some controversy, but it did set them thinking. One girl claimed that her father had a forked twig sucked from his neck. He was seriously ill at the time and they began to welcome some of Shirley's medicine as back up to their own beliefs. One of the shamans had been suffering with malaria for some time and another shaman claimed to have sucked out a piece of cardboard from his forehead which he declared to be the cause of his sickness. In practice, there was no serious conflict with the shaman. He would suck out the 'sickness seed' which he believed was the cause of the illness. He might also indicate local remedies to treat the symptoms. Shirley had brought, what appeared to be, more effective remedies and he was not averse to taking them.

There were many fears. They seemed to be very afraid of being in the jungle at night although they would go through it in the daytime with no problem. Their concerns appeared to be much more than that of meeting some animal along the way. They were afraid too of the spirits of the dead, and would keep well away from the burial areas. By nature the Paumarí were a timid people, preferring to flee from danger rather than stay and face it, unless they were drunk. Fear of rejection was a torment to them, and they would often send someone else to ask a favour rather than take the risk of having their request refused. For many of them, fear was crippling. The message about Jesus and His power over evil spirits was certainly good news. It was already clear that opposing spiritual forces had been stirred. Shirley and Mary Ann often felt a real sense of oppression.

There was one shaman for each extended family and they were feared by the people. They knew that he could put curses on them. In general, his intentions were benevolent, although his methods were considerably influenced by tradition, ignorance and also the occult. In general, Shirley had a reasonable relationship with the shamans.

Traditions surrounding health and hygiene were a challenge. Early on Shirley introduced the principle of using a clean blade to cut the cord of a newborn baby, rather than any knife which might be to hand. Almost immediately, the incidents of newborn tetanus decreased dramatically. It had been fairly common for mothers to lose their babies at birth or when they were very small, and as a result they did not make any clothes for it until after the birth. What would be the point, they reasoned, in having clothes but no baby? Shirley and Mary Ann started to give a baby blanket and a small piece of cloth at each delivery. They also gave the new mother a cup of rice and a tin of powdered milk which was for the building up of her own strength.

On one occasion Shirley was offered a baby to keep when
she had delivered it. The mother was a lady who had
Hansen's disease (leprosy). Shirley knew her quite well as
she was one of a number with the disease that she had been
treating for some time. The Paumarí were never known
to have the disease themselves but, nevertheless, stigma
surrounding the condition was widespread. The lady did not
live in their village, but the local midwife was scared to help.
When the time came for her baby to be born, Shirley was
called to deliver it. It was a bittersweet time. The little boy
was born fit and well and the delivery was straightforward.
The mother had already lost her fingers and toes to the
disease. It was hard to know how she would cope. The
mother obviously thought the same. Shirley declined as
graciously as she could. She wondered what the director
would say if she reappeared in Porto Velho with a child in
tow, and was firm in her resolve that there was enough to do,
without opening a children's home as well!

It was not hard to understand the stigma surrounding some
illnesses but it was extremely difficult to explain the cause
and effect of disease when much of it was invisible. It could
have taken a lifetime to explain about contaminated water,
poor and unbalanced diet, bacteria and viruses and so on.
How could she explain that a tiny mosquito could cause
malaria? Why should it make sense that not all mosquitoes
would carry disease, only some of them? Mothers found it
particularly hard to understand dehydration in their babies.
To their way of thinking, if the baby was vomiting or had
diarrhoea they should give nothing, otherwise it would make
it vomit even more. A visual aid proved useful. Shirley held
up a plastic bag which she had filled with water, and around
the centre of which was drawn a line. She explained that this
was like the fluid in a baby. If the level of water went below
the line, the baby would die. By making some puncture
holes in the lower half of the bag, the mothers could see

how the fluid could become dangerously low if the baby was vomiting or had diarrhoea. Shirley showed them that if fluid was still being lost, they needed to add to it, even a few drops at a time.

The Paumarí were not the only ones who had health problems. A splinter of wood had got under Shirley's toe nail. One of the Paumarí managed to get it out for her but within hours her leg was twice its normal size. Realizing the potential seriousness of any infection, Mary Ann called the centre to request that the plane come for them. However, it was being used by some government officials who were going to make a brief visit to the Paumarí village. On arrival, and on seeing Shirley's leg, they insisted that they themselves should stay in the village and that the pilot should take Shirley back to Porto Velho. There was not enough room for them all. It must have been quite an experience for them to spend a night in Shirley's village home.

In the meantime, Shirley was taken to a doctor in town. Unfortunately, his consulting room was on the first floor. By then, her leg was enormous and she found it impossible to climb the stairs, even though she tried to crawl up them. Eventually, a colleague carried her up. The doctor was extremely concerned and wondered if she might have tetanus. He prescribed a full course of vaccine against tetanus and two lots of strong antibiotics. A colleague who gave the injections into Shirley's arm was alarmed at the localised reaction which caused huge swelling. However, in due course all the medication was effective and Shirley was able to return to the village.

One day a Brazilian woman arrived with her baby who was very sick. She had heard that Shirley was a nurse and was desperate for help. The child needed some regular injections but there was no one suitable in the lady's village to administer them. Shirley suggested that if she came back every day, then she herself would give them to the baby. The mother was a lady of substantial build and she explained to Shirley that she needed an extra large canoe in which to travel. She did not think that there would be one available on a daily basis.

More than a week passed before Shirley saw her again. The baby was better, but her older child was now acting strangely and being very uncommunicative. The mother had taken the baby to an occult healer and this had been the result. Shirley began to share something of the power of God and how He could change people's lives. The older child began to run her fingers along a necklace she was wearing. She seemed uncomfortable. Suddenly she ripped it off and she was instantly set free of whatever it was that was afflicting her. The power of God was being demonstrated.

Some days were extraordinary; some were normal, whatever that was. Some were discouraging and others had moments when a villager suddenly understood a truth for the first time and applied it to life. Those days were special indeed. Despite people always being around, there were moments when Shirley felt intense loneliness. There were times when the sense of spiritual oppression was intense and it was a real personal battle to fight through. But through it all, there was a deep reality within her that God was with her and that His grace and strength would be sufficient for everything she needed.

In addition to her own translation work, Mary Ann gave a great deal of practical support. She was always willing to hold the head of a dental patient or boil up instruments in readiness for another session of pulling teeth. She was sensitive to the fact that Shirley's back gave her pain from time to time and would take over the sweeping and other jobs which aggravated it. She had a real vision for the Paumarí to get more involved in trade. They would buy baskets from the Paumarí to encourage this idea, and then take them out to Porto Velho to sell on. Mary Ann commended them for their natural talent but encouraged them to use more than one colour and to improve on design and quality. She gave them vision and encouraged them in it.

Preparing farinha

10 The pine cone

On one of the return trips to the village, Buster was not around to greet the plane. He, along with the whole of the dog population, had succumbed to distemper. However, life was seldom without some extra residents, human or otherwise.

Rascal was another pet who came to live with them. He belonged to the pilot and his family but they were going on home leave for a year. The plan was to bring him in on the float plane when Shirley and Mary Ann returned to the village. However, Rascal escaped just before take off and went for a swim. He got thoroughly muddy in the process and there was no way to clean him up. He was hauled aboard and sat beside Mary Ann. But when the pilot revved the engine, Rascal had a panic attack. He leapt onto Mary Ann, climbed on her lap and shook violently. He put his filthy paws on her shoulders and refused to leave her for the whole flight. Who was the more muddy when they emerged, Mary Ann or Rascal? It was very hard to tell.

Because of his size Rascal immediately became the pack leader among the village dogs and lived up to his name. However, he hated not having his usual toilet facilities in the wet season and took to using any canoe which was tied up at the door.

Other animals came and went. A neighbour's cat used to accompany Shirley on her walks into the jungle. A wild baby turkey and a racoon came to stay for a while, but both were insanely jealous of each other and fought over who would sit the closest to Shirley's feet as she studied. A baby toucan was also given hospitality for a while and particularly enjoyed eating açai fruit which were the size of aniseed balls. Later on it would regurgitate them and the resulting effect was like a game of marbles. Baby-sitting animals was never dull!

Hungry humans presented more of a dilemma. Toinia was a 4 year old orphan who sometimes came and sat just a couple of yards away from the table, waiting for a little food. Benjamin often arrived at breakfast time and hoped for a cup of coffee. He was one of the older men in the village. He also hoped that he might get some food. Segundo, a former shaman, was both old and blind and often came around at mealtimes, especially when his own relatives did not have any food.

What was the answer to these situations? If the Paumarí had no fish they often had nothing to eat. If Shirley and Mary Ann had food what should they do? Should they feed them? But what about others who would start to come for food too? Was it their mission to feed the whole village? Who would pay for all the extra food? How would they get it there? How many flights would it involve? Was it right to give endlessly? Were medical and dental help, literacy and language not enough? Should the Paumarí not give a bit more thought into planning for another day? Why did they not plant more manioc? Why did they do some of the things which they did?

These and many other questions flew round and round Shirley's mind as she attended an anthropological workshop in Porto Velho. It was time to take an objective look at the Paumarí way of life and the problems they faced. It was also time to reflect on her own part in the overall picture, and to consider how best to react to some of the day to day situations which arose. It would be so easy to get caught up with the endless problems of survival, and miss the purpose for which she was there.

FUNAI existed to support the Indians and their land rights. Issues such as economics and health were also their responsibility. In addition to FUNAI, there were other non-governmental organisations with an interest. Relationships with these groups, and their feelings and respect for SIL work depended to a large degree on the people who were working for the organisations at the time. Not all of them were sympathetic to the spread of the gospel, and whilst some individuals were extremely helpful, others seemed to have less honourable and even subversive motives. Others would use individuals to suit their own ends whilst being against them in principle.

It was about this time that Meinke Salzer came to work with the Paumarí. She had previously been working with a different indigenous group but permission to remain there had been refused. Meinke had a Brazilian mother and German father, and had spent time in both countries during her childhood. She had been to Bible College in Switzerland and went to England to study English. Along with her fluent Portuguese, German and English, she had studied a number of the indigenous languages. Meinke was a trained nurse and immediately got stuck into the endless stream of patients who needed help.

There was always plenty of medical work. They housed a fellow for two weeks who had severe chest burns having fallen drunk into a fire. It gave a new meaning to the word hospital-ity. Another had severe head injuries after a drunken brawl. Two men became paralysed and had severe anaemia. One refused help and died shortly after. The medicines he had been given were found untouched after his death. His wife said he believed that someone had put a curse on him, so there was no point in taking them. The other paralysed man was taken to Porto Velho but he never regained the use of his legs. An outbreak of flu left several babies critically ill, but in each case God had mercy on them. They all survived. So it went on... dramatic illness and accident... everyday illness and crisis. No two days were ever the same.

A lady came with a large sebaceous cyst on her head which was a horribly infected mass. It needed to be opened, cleaned and stitched, but Shirley was not sure whether it was something she should tackle. She sent a message to a doctor colleague asking for advice. The patient was distressed and as time went by, Shirley felt that she had no option but to do the best she could for her. She set to work and was relatively satisfied with the result. Some time after that she had a response to her earlier message. "Do not touch that head!" It was a bit late by then.

Shirley started one letter to her supporters with a question. Can you eat an elephant? The answer to that might be that to eat it in one go was impossible, but if it was cut up into small pieces and eaten over a long period of time then it might be manageable. In some ways the huge challenge of translating the scriptures was an equally daunting prospect. The initial project was to translate the New Testament, but other books and subjects kept popping into Shirley's mind as she could see how they would relate to the Paumarí and help their understanding of the gospel.

During these years various works were started, completed or in process. The book of Acts and Genesis, a large part of Exodus, some of Joshua, 1 Samuel, stories of Elijah, Elisha and Daniel together with the books of Ruth and Esther. Galatians was in its first draft. Much of these works had been revised and fine-tuned along the way. Key words had been checked and major concepts agreed upon with translation consultants.

Once the first draft had been written and revised, then checked again with different language helpers, the material was carefully typed onto a stencil ready to be duplicated on a mimeograph machine. With the stencil wrapped around an ink filled drum, it was then turned, either by hand or by electricity to reproduce the sheet. Mistakes made on a stencil were not easy to alter, and getting it to sit neatly on the drum also had its tricky moments. The whole process could be very messy.

When photocopiers later became available there were both advantages and disadvantages. Although the process was easier, the quality could still be variable. After each book was completed it was read aloud informally in the evenings. Those who could read were given copies to take home.

With the sale of the family home back in England complete, Shirley was able to ask for a small house to be built on the Porto Velho centre. As much as she loved her friends and colleagues, a place of her own was pure bliss. The many medical calls on her time no longer added a burden to Mary Ann. Dishes and dust could wait until she was ready to tackle domestic chores.

She was certainly being called on more and more when she was on the centre. It took a lot of time and energy to walk around in the hot sun. She decided to buy a bicycle, but there did not seem to be any in the local shops. One day, when she and Mary Ann were shopping for groceries, Shirley heard that a large consignment of bicycles had just been delivered in town. Not wanting to waste a moment, she left Mary Ann to pay the bill for her shopping, and hurried off to the bike shop. There were some lovely bikes for sale and she was just about to buy one, when a colleague came rather breathlessly into the shop.

She seemed quite angry that Shirley was there. Her attitude was rather upsetting. Shirley could not understand it, and decided to leave the shop and come back another time. She just hoped that there would still be some bikes for sale. When she arrived back at her house, there, in the middle of the sitting room was a lovely red bicycle, shining and brand new. It was a present from her colleagues for all medical work which she did among them. The colleague who had been in the shop was the one who was there to prevent Shirley from buying a second bicycle. What a relief it was to have the misunderstanding resolved, and she was certainly delighted with the thoughtfulness of their present to her.

The time came for some more home leave. With it came the request that she should teach at a linguistics course again. Life, as always, had been extremely busy. Sometime around the middle of the course the organisers realised that they had one more member of staff than they needed and decided that Shirley was the one most in need of a break. She suddenly found herself with a week off, but with no plans.

As she made her way back to the living quarters, she wondered what to do with this surprise break. It would be good to get away and have a complete change of scenery and to be refreshed in body and mind, but she wondered where to go. It was such short notice and part of the fun of a holiday was to plan and anticipate being with friends. Although it was a lovely offer, it also presented a dilemma, with decisions needing to be made immediately if she was going to benefit from the opportunity.

She stopped briefly to chat with one of the students and the conversation was such a surprise. The student had been asked to arrange a holiday for someone who was coming over to England, and who was not now able to come. So she had a place booked at a holiday retreat somewhere near Blackpool, but no one to take it! It seemed remarkable.

As Shirley set off for her free holiday, her mind was full of anticipation. She knew that God was behind it all and she wondered just what He had in store for her. She arrived and settled in, and it was good to enjoy the services with no personal responsibility for them. The first day came and went with no particularly special moments, but Shirley was so full of anticipation and did not mind a bit. Her special moment would most definitely come. She knew that.

As the week went on she began to feel a little flat. She knew that God had brought her here, but nothing special had stood out for her. She wondered what it was all about. The final meeting of the week arrived, and then ended, still with nothing special for her. She was disappointed. Just then, she heard the speaker mention a basket of pine cones which were at the back. She suggested that each person take one as they left the hall, and consider what it represented in their lives.

Outside in the grounds a huge bonfire had been lit. It was the time of Christian marches across the country with bonfires being lit in strategic places, and this was one of them. The speaker went on to suggest that once they knew what the pine cone represented in their lives, that they should throw it on the fire, symbolically giving it back to God in surrender. Shirley got up from the meeting and made her way out. She had absolutely no idea what a pine cone might mean in her life. She could not understand what this week had all been about. However, she dutifully picked up a pine cone from the basket and followed the other people as they left the hall.

The fire was blazing well, and the wood crackled. Sparks flew high into the night sky. A light breeze was blowing and the flames danced in the wind. People stood around watching and chatting, and by now most of them had thrown their cone into the fire and were just enjoying the atmosphere of the bonfire. Shirley stood silently, away from the group. In her heart she was asking God to show her the meaning of her pine cone.

As she waited, she had a real sense that what she held in her hand represented her life with the Paumarí. She was shocked and confused. In what way, she wondered? Was she to spend her whole life there? Would she die out there with them? Was there something else? She did not know. She turned the pine cone over carefully as she considered the challenge before her. Her work with the Paumarí represented her whole life. There had been so much training.

She thought back to the years working with Mary Ann. The task before them had often seemed overwhelming but there was no doubt that they had made progress. The villagers were learning to read and the translation work was well under way. Countless lives had been saved through the medical help they had been able to give. Was God asking her to give it all up? What would be the point of that? She remembered back to the day when she had decided to follow Jesus, and when she had surrendered her life to Him. What was He asking of her now? The challenge seemed to burn within her as hot as the fire before her. Could she, would she, surrender her pine cone to the flames, giving God the right, as it were, to take it all away if that was what He wanted.

She did not know how long she stood there. The other people had started to sing but she barely heard them. She knew that this was a significant moment and yet it had taken her by surprise. She had been anticipating a special encounter all week, and although she had not known what to expect, it was certainly not this. But as the moments ticked by, she knew what she had to do. A walk of faith was all about surrendering to the will of God. She had come to understand that surrender to God is not the weak option, but is actually a huge step of faith into the safest place that we can be. Although she thought that she had surrendered her life to God before, if He was asking it of her again now, perhaps even literally, then that was the answer. If her identity was somehow linked to the Paumarí, she would let it go and trust once more that her security and significance were in God alone. It was a challenge and yet, on the other hand, she knew that there was really no debate. She threw the pine cone and stood watching as it was swallowed up in the flames.

She did not want to talk to anyone at that moment, so slipped quietly back into the hall. The lights were out now, but the bonfire cast shadows on the walls. Two candles burned at the front. She sat down at the back and started to pray. The silence seemed to surround her with peace and as she waited, she felt God impress a picture in her mind of a man sitting in an armchair, and a little girl going across to climb up onto her daddy's lap. The child snuggled up close and put her arms around her father's neck. Silently, the father put his arms around her and they were together, in perfect security and harmony. She felt God speak into her heart:

"That's all it is. My loving you and you loving Me."

It was a moment on holy ground. In that instant she knew that whatever the pine cone represented, God's love would be sufficient.

When the time came to consider her return to Brazil there was no tussle in her spirit. There was no conviction that she should not go, just the real sense of a job to be done and a calling to do it. So God had not asked her to give up her work with the Paumarí. What He had asked was for her to be willing either way.

The demands on her financial resources were still considerable, and she fairly regularly needed to receive from the emergency fund to top up. She felt God challenge her on this. She was horrified. How would she supply all the medicines which she used, on her regular amount of gifts? But the sense of God's challenge was insistent. She thought of the verse which says, "And God will generously provide all you need. Then you will always have everything you need and plenty left over to share with others. As the Scriptures say, They share freely and give generously to the poor. Their good deeds will be remembered forever."[17] Would she allow God complete control over her finances? Could He put His hand freely in her pocket for others?

Once again though, there was no real battle. Although she was shocked by the challenge, there it was and it needed a response. She decided there and then that she would never again receive from the emergency fund. Once she had made the decision, she never needed it. There was always enough. God had proved Himself once more.

[17] *2 Corinthians 9:8-9 (NLT)*

Back in the village some months later she went on an afternoon walk. They had managed to persuade the Paumarí to allow them a siesta, but sometimes Shirley preferred to slip quietly into the jungle and walk alone. A huge bumblebee seemed to follow her. She was not frightened of it particularly but to the Paumarí, a bee brought a message from the shaman. It was a big thing for them, and as she walked along she pondered that and the many other beliefs which they had.

As she paused to rest, the bee paused too. She thought about how a bee can only sting once, and gives its life in the process. She thought about death, and how that Jesus Himself had come to take the sting of death from the believer. As she got up and continued her walk back to the village, a wave of peace settled on her once more. Whilst she might give all her energy to the Paumarí and her vision for them, God was reminding her that her own future was safe with Him. With the pine cone He had reminded her of His presence and availability in this life, and through the bee had spoken to her of security in the life to come, whenever that might be.

Shirley had often spoken words over to herself whenever she stepped into the float plane, and remembered them again now. "If we live, we live to the Lord, and if we die, we die to the Lord. So then, whether we live or we die, we belong to the Lord."[18] It was win, win, all the way.

Shirley was shocked to learn of Jumper's serious deterioration in health and desperately saddened when she died. Gisi had remarried, this time to a Paumarí man, but this left Fátima in a difficult position. She could hardly sleep in the same mosquito net as her sister and brother-in-law, but it was not safe for her to be alone outside. It was not long before she was married off to one of the teenage boys, but the arrangement did not last for long.

[18] *Romans 14:8 (Amplified Bible)*

Fátima was in Porto Velho helping at a workshop when her first baby was due. In spite of numerous difficulties Zefinha was born alive and well. Fátima had problems with subsequent deliveries and two babies did not survive.

Shirley often thought about the group of Paumarí who lived on the Tapauá River. She longed to visit them and assess their needs. She and Mary Ann made plans, and arranged with the pilot to take them on the one hour flight. If they went by canoe with outboard motor, it would take seven days. The pilot dropped them off and made arrangements to come back and pick them up two weeks later. As the people came out to meet these two white women, they were amazed to discover that their visitors spoke Paumarí. Their faces said it all.

The villagers made them welcome and found space for them in a house. But living conditions were even more basic than in their own Paumarí village of Maraha. The house was extremely rickety and the central board was most unstable. The tallest man in the village seemed to be no higher than Shirley herself and many of the people were considerably shorter, so their living accommodation was built accordingly. Shirley and Mary Ann kept knocking their heads on the roof supports. There were no walls to the house at all. Life was back to public view. Neither was there any hole in the ground, so toilet facilities were even more primitive than usual.

They had left their two-way radio with Meinke and had brought a spare, but it was disconcerting to discover that it did not work. They had no contact at all with the outside world. They realised that Meinke and other colleagues would be worried about them, but there was absolutely nothing they could do about it.

The village was tiny with just four dwellings and a couple of raft houses. The only contact the villagers had with the outside world was with passing river traders. The children no longer spoke Paumarí, but their mastery of Portuguese was very limited. Some of the teenage boys could hardly string a sentence together. It was very sad.

As Shirley and Mary Ann spent time with them, they compared the dialects between the two villages. The cultures were only slightly different but there was no contact between the two groups. Their pottery making was good and they certainly had a skill which the Paumarí in Maraha did not possess.

Ten days later they heard the sound of the plane landing on the lake. The pilot had been concerned at the lack of contact and had decided to come earlier than anticipated to pick them up. They were not sorry to see him.

As they gathered up their few belongings and climbed on board, it was with mixed feelings. There were so many needs in this remote place but it would need much reflection to consider how best to help them in the future.

Life settled back into some sort of routine until the early hours of one morning when Shirley and Mary Ann were disturbed by loud shouting. In an instant they were wide awake. They grabbed a torch and stumbled out to see the cause of the commotion.

A group of Paumarí men were outside the house, agitated and breathless. To begin with, it was hard to make sense of what they were saying. After a few minutes the men calmed down enough to explain that they had seen a big Brazilian boat full of soldiers coming in the direction of the village. Their own history of massacre had left them very suspicious of anyone in uniform but this time they were not so much concerned for themselves. Their terror was on behalf of Shirley and Mary Ann. They were petrified that the ladies were about to be abducted by terrorists.

Shirley and Mary Ann hastily got dressed. The possibility of abduction or kidnap had certainly crossed their minds from

time to time and they took the threat very seriously. They
tried to get on the radio to Porto Velho but the atmospheric
conditions were not good at that time of the morning and
there was no response. Just then, a voice came through the
receiver. It was one of SIL's radio men who were working in
Belem on the far side of the country, hundreds of miles away.
Amazingly it was he who had received the call. He assured
them that he would contact the team in Porto Velho by
whatever means he could.

The Paumarí men were urging them to flee into the jungle
so that they would not be caught, but they decided to stay
and face the situation head on. They did, however, quickly
put together a bag of essential items just in case. It was hard
to know what one might need in the case of kidnap, but
a torch would always come in handy. A change of clothes,
some paper and a pen, a Bible and a few medicines were
squeezed in. Shirley quickly went into the bedroom to pray.
The situation was very frightening and yet, as she paused in
the midst of the panic to commit her life once more to God,
an overwhelming peace swept over her.

When the boat arrived, soldiers armed with machine guns
surrounded the house. A few Paumarí men who were inside
the house were not allowed to leave. Those outside were
not allowed in. A few soldiers came in and asked to see their
documents. They wanted proof that Shirley and Mary Ann
had permission to be in the country. In addition, they wanted
evidence that FUNAI knew they were there. They looked at
the two-way radio and asked for the documents which gave
the authority for them to use it. All the papers were in order.

They searched the house and at one point found an old shot
gun. Shirley held her breath as they examined it closely and
whispered amongst themselves. One of the Paumarí had
asked Shirley if she would take it to Porto Velho next time she
went and get it repaired for him. It seemed a long time that

the soldiers held it, turning it over and over in their hands. Shirley wondered if they believed her story or not.

To her relief they put the gun down and expressed disgust that anyone would even think of using such an old weapon. They finally said that they were satisfied all the documents were in order and began to leave. The situation had become quite surreal. Shirley offered them coffee which they refused. Then they were gone. Once the boat had pulled away and the tension had eased, there were plenty of other people who definitely did need a cup.

11 Valleys

Her face was white and drawn and there was no response as Shirley felt once more for the erratic pulse. It seemed as though events had taken over again so quickly. Was it really only fifteen minutes before that she had found Meinke, huddled and shivering under a pile of clothes inside the mosquito net? She had placed a thermometer under her arm, although there was no question in her mind that Meinke had another high fever. Even so, she was shocked to see how high the mercury had risen, touching just over 107°F (41.5°C). Even as she stared at it in disbelief, Meinke's back arched in a convulsion. An intravenous injection of Dipirona had helped bring the temperature down, but now she lay there, hanging to life by a thread. Twice she opened her eyes briefly in a glassy, unrecognising stare, and then shut them again. There was no other response.

It was Wednesday evening and Shirley's mind went back to the previous Saturday night. She and Mary Ann had sat beside Meinke then in another battle for life. It had been 65 hours since her kidneys had functioned and having done all she could medically, there was nothing else to do but sit and pray. They read some of the Psalms aloud, and just occasionally there had been a momentary flicker of response from Meinke as the words of hope touched her. But the battle was intense. It felt as though some deep, dark forces wanted to pull her away from this life and into the beyond.

Eventually – and amazingly – Meinke's kidneys did start to function again. It could only be by the grace of God. Sunday had been a poor day with various lesser crises, and a return of the malaria. It was a particularly severe attack.

Here they were now at the ninth potentially fatal crisis in the last few days. Would God intervene once more? Shirley and Meinke both believed for healing and two days before, Shirley had felt touched again by the words from John's gospel, "And I will do whatever you ask in My name, so that the Son may bring glory to the Father."[19] She and Meinke had asked together for healing. Now she lay semi-conscious.

Since the drama had begun, Shirley had been almost tormented by panic. Outwardly she was calm and composed, but inwardly she was terrified at what the next crisis might be and how she would respond. Medically speaking, there was nothing left that she could do. Each new emergency brought fresh fear. There was spiritual tension too. She felt unwilling to let Meinke's life be taken, and hung onto the promises of God.

A month previously she had been reading the story of the parable of the sower, and had been challenged by some words. "The one who received the seed that fell among the thorns is the one who hears the word, but the worries of this life and the deceitfulness of wealth choke it, making it unfruitful."[20] She did not feel that 'deceitfulness of wealth' was an issue in her life, but it had been quite a shock to be reminded that worry could have such a devastating effect. It could steal her peace and leave her spiritually empty. She was reminded again of the words that Peter wrote to the churches, encouraging them to "Give all your worries and cares to God, for He cares about you."[21] She had shared such truths with the Paumarí, but although it sounded easy, the reality was often very different. She wondered if worry could actually be a sin, and that the Lord was grieved when she continued to struggle with burdens when He wanted to carry the load. It was challenging.

Shirley realised that she must release Meinke to God's will. Yes, she believed passionately for healing, but it was time to

[19] *John 14:13 New International Version (NIV ©1984)*
[20] *Mark 4:19 (NIV ©1984)*
[21] *1 Peter 5:7 (NLT)*

offer her friend back to God, giving Him the right to heal her or take her, as He chose.

"Lord, if she is not going to be mentally normal as a result of this, please do not hear our prayer to spare her life." Peace now returned.

Meinke's feet were icy cold and they struggled to get them warm. Two of the language helpers sat silently with them. Their children were asleep on the floor. Shirley prayed inwardly as they waited.

Suddenly, with no warning, Meinke sat up! She immediately asked for some food.

"Why can't I have some food? I'm hungry." Shirley was shocked at the dramatic change but instinctively passed her a glass of water. Meinke took a long drink and repeated her plea for something to eat. Two hours earlier she had been unable to swallow. But now there was no reason why she should not eat. She was better. Everything was normal!

Shirley hardly knew whether to laugh or cry. She could almost hear the words of Jesus as He spoke to Jairus after having raised his daughter from the dead, as He directed that she should be given something to eat.[22]

There was no medical explanation for the sudden healing. It could only have been the power of God. It was exciting that a few of the Paumarí had witnessed the moment when Meinke recovered so rapidly, and word spread among them of the miracle which only God could do. As they reflected the following day on what had happened, Meinke commented that she had heard the Psalms being read, and how the words had calmed her even though she could not respond.

The year brought many other challenges. One of the non-governmental agencies began to stir up indigenous people groups to claim their land rights. Some of them visited the

[22] *Luke 8:55b (Amplified Bible)*

Paumarí to present their radical ideas. There was a sense of trouble ahead. Quite by chance, Shirley found that a lawsuit had been started against her.

A group of Dutch missionaries had been doing some exploratory visits to the area and were working on plans for a centre some thirty minutes canoe ride away from the village. It would be staffed mostly by Brazilians but funded from Holland. Plans were in hand for medical work, literacy, economic and social help for the local people. To get them started, Meinke was to spend three months with them, teaching their nurse about local diseases. Shirley would give some advice on midwifery and dentistry.

The Dutch pastor was implementing the project and had gone to Lábrea for discussions with various officials, including the local judge. It was during the meeting that the pastor discovered a legal case had been opened against Shirley, with the purpose of expelling her from the land on which her house was built. The person who was generally considered to be the land owner was behind this action.

Shirley was shocked. She herself had not been informed and had the Dutch pastor not been talking to the judge, she wondered how long it might have been before anyone would have thought to tell her. It seemed that the local head of Indian affairs considered that the land belonged to the Paumarí, but there was a real power struggle in progress.

A whole series of wild charges had been brought with regard to them teaching English and destroying the religious culture. The judge appeared to know very little about the Dutch mission team or SIL, other than odd scraps he might have read in the papers. It seemed though that his mind was already made up and that there was little chance of them winning the case.

Further implications to the case would involve the Paumarí directly. If land ownership was proved then it was only one step further before he could force the Paumarí out too.

Apoena Meirelles, the local FUNAI representative, was really concerned. It brought to the surface the need for the whole question of land rights to be resolved.

Shirley was advised that she must contest the case otherwise it would be taken as clear evidence of guilt. Apoena visited the village and seemed impressed with what he saw. FUNAI wanted to confirm on a map which area the Paumarí considered their own. Shirley was offered their lawyer as they were keen to represent her. The land rights for the Indians were the focus of their department.

The case rumbled on for months. Other rumours surfaced and, in addition to the false accusations, Shirley discovered that there was also a claim for damages which she was supposed to have caused the land owner. Political agitators were very active, stirring up trouble and at times, pretending to be associated with the SIL work. They would go into an area and ride on the back of the good work which was already being done, then leave and cause mayhem from a distance. There was more going on behind the scenes than just the question of land ownership.

The uncertainties caused an uneasy atmosphere. Without agreement on the land, the Dutch group could not go ahead with their plans. In the meantime they would work from Lábrea and buy an uncontested piece of land further upriver to establish a clinic.

These were not the only changes. For some while there had been restrictions on people working in the indigenous areas. Strict regulations limited the use of planes and radios. It was all becoming very difficult. Some of the SIL teams found it impossible to get new or renewed visas. It was extremely frustrating to have the work held up. It was true that some could be done in Porto Velho but so much more needed to happen alongside local people and language helpers. It felt as though the door of opportunity into the villages was beginning to close.

Meinke had been unwell for several days and on the previous evening she had been resting on the bed while Shirley hung the mosquito nets. She had spoken very quietly.

"Shirley," her voice barely audible. "My jaw is getting stiff and a few minutes ago I couldn't open my mouth or talk. It feels very strange."

Tetanus! Lockjaw. The diagnosis was not difficult but it sent a shiver down Shirley's spine. They were in the village a day away from Lábrea. Because of the new restrictions, they were not allowed to use the radio. There was no transportation and not enough antitoxin to complete a treatment. Shirley's mind raced back through the last few days. Meinke had got a thorn in her foot which they had not been able to get out, but they did not realise there was an infection. In addition to antitoxin she needed penicillin, but was very allergic to it. Once again Shirley sent an emergency SOS prayer. "In my desperation I prayed, and the Lord listened; He saved me from all my troubles."[23]

Before she had time to give an injection, Meinke was having the first of several painful convulsions. Shirley gave all the antitoxin which she had, but it was only about a third of the recommended dose. Meinke's condition improved immediately but they knew that the situation was serious. Shirley hurriedly wrote a note to a local Brazilian who might have some antitoxin. They had sold him an ampoule several months before. Two Paumarí men set off immediately to take the note. The wind was howling and the rain lashing down as they left the house and disappeared into the darkness. Shirley was grateful that they did not hesitate. It would be a terrifying trip for anyone in the storm. Meinke began to shiver and shake with a mild reaction to the medicine. It was a long, restless night.

It seemed urgent that they get to Lábrea with access to more antitoxin and advanced medical treatment. As Shirley did what nursing care she could, she prayed as she worked.

[23] *Psalm 34:6 (NLT)*

"Lord, I believe it is the right thing to go downriver to Lábrea. We don't have any transportation and we don't have time to go looking. If you want us to go, please would you arrange a boat for us?" It was one of those desperate sorts of prayers without fancy trimmings. It was a matter of life or death. But Shirley had seen God answer in critical situations before, and now she turned to Him again.

The two Paumarí men returned with a single ampoule and a note saying that the Brazilian would come by in the morning. He kept his word and not only came, but also went to several other villages looking to see if anyone else had some antitoxin. He also promised to look for someone with a motor boat to help them. By midday it was obvious that there was no more antitoxin available.

The morning had been relatively quiet in the village but by lunchtime it began to get busy. The house was starting to fill up with people, and around and about outside there seemed endless noise. Dogs were barking, children were crying and people calling to one another. It was nothing out of the ordinary – just normal everyday life. But inside the bedroom every noise seemed magnified and brought with it the threat of further convulsions.

The light from a single lamp on the table lit up the faces of the Paumarí who sat on the benches lining the walls. They waited anxiously while Shirley and Mary Ann moved quietly back and forth in the dark trying to complete the packing and shut up the house. It all seemed like an impossible nightmare. Twenty four hours had now passed since it all began.

It was eight in the evening when they heard the sound of an outboard motor coming along the lake. The Brazilian had found a big canoe with an outboard motor and someone willing to take them downriver. Before completing his arrangements, however, he had heard of a big, fast boat which was about to leave. He had hurriedly gone to ask the captain of the government boat if he was willing to wait. Helpful hands now carried the sundry boxes and bags down to the canoe. It was pitch black and slippery after the rain.

Strong men attached the hammock to poles and carried Meinke carefully down the steps of the house and towards the lake. Had she been aware of what was happening she might have felt like the product of a hunting trip, but she was past caring. It was steep and slippery and there were many stumbles on the way. Progress was slow. Would the captain wait for them on the river? The carriers eventually placed Meinke in the canoe. Shirley and Mary Ann squeezed in beside her. It was the low water season and the strip of water connecting the lake to the river was dangerous with numerous submerged trees in the swirling waters. Small silver fish jumped all around them and sometimes landed in the canoe. Shirley sent up another urgent SOS prayer.

"Lord. Please help us."

As the lake reached the main river, the boat was waiting. It was nothing short of a miracle for such a big boat to be there in the low water. It was not just any old boat either. It was a boat with a roof over their heads and bunks to lie on. Shirley gave Meinke some sedative to help minimise the effects of the noise and vibrations from the powerful motor as they sped downriver to Lábrea. By morning they were safely docked and Shirley hurried ashore to find a shop selling antitoxin. With the medicine in hand she then went to the home of their good friend, the pastor of the local church. She quickly told him the story and hurried back to the boat to give the medicine.

The crisis was by no means over, but now there were others to help. The pastor took them into his home and helping hands appeared from everywhere. The most urgent need was to get a message to the pilot in Porto Velho. The pastor contacted his brother by phone. He worked in Porto Velho and quickly took a taxi the seven miles to the centre.

Meanwhile, Meinke was battling with another severe reaction
to the antitoxin. Shirley wondered if she dare give more to
complete the treatment? The plane arrived with a minimum
of delay and the pilot soon had an improvised bed made
up. But would Meinke survive the journey? She struggled
to breathe as they watched anxiously for another injection
to take effect and relax the convulsion. Many hands helped
carry Meinke gently to the plane. As they landed in Porto
Velho, colleagues were waiting for them with a car and more
medicine. It was necessary to give this as they went along.

The time it had taken from village to centre was an all-time
record. There had been a minimum of delay and trouble.
God had provided a canoe, boat, taxi, plane and car, friends,
strangers and colleagues, medicines and everything they
needed. Once again they proved that even though they
walked through the valley of the shadow of death, His hand
had provided.

These times when Meinke's life hung in the balance posed
many dilemmas for Shirley. There was the responsibility of
making and taking decisions on her behalf with regard to
diagnosis and treatment. There were her own emotions
at seeing her friend so sick. There was the desire to set a
good example to the Paumarí in terms of response in prayer
and faith. In addition, those in the SIL leadership had a
responsibility to their workers, and Shirley needed to be
accountable to them and to inform them when there was a
serious problem. But she also knew Meinke's heart, which
was so committed to the work which God had called her to
do, and her reluctance to leave it. Many were the times that
Shirley watched as Meinke swung gently in the hammock,
still burning with fever, but with a language helper sitting
beside her as they continued to work. There had been times
too when Meinke had come back from a semi-conscious
state only to get up and go straight back to work at her desk.

Here was the truth of God's word in action. Paul spoke to the Corinthian church these words: "However, we possess this precious treasure (the divine light of the gospel) in (frail, human) vessels of earth, that the grandeur and exceeding greatness of the power may be shown to be from God and not from ourselves".[24] Paul spoke too of us being more than conquerors through Him that loved us. Yes – we can conquer mountains or difficult circumstances or whatever, but for the child of God there is a power within them given by the presence of the Holy Spirit which makes them more than a conqueror.[25]

Meinke's life demonstrated these truths more eloquently than any words as the reality of a life committed to God and His power shone through the broken vessel of her sick body. The Paumarí saw the power of God's word demonstrated in action time and time again.

The SIL director called a meeting of Shirley, Mary Ann and Meinke. He told Mary Ann that he would like her to leave the village work and change assignment. He wanted her to be his secretary in Brasilia. There had been no indication that this plan was in the pipeline and it came as something of a shock. The Paumarí would be distressed, Shirley thought, as they were very fond of Mary Ann. She herself would never have been able to achieve what she had done without Mary Ann's support.

He then turned to Meinke. His suggestion was that Meinke should return to her home in the south of Brazil for a year to get fully fit. In addition to severe malaria and tetanus, she had also suffered from filariasis. As they emerged from the meeting there were many emotions.

Soon after that, authorisation for all the teams to travel in the interior was completely withdrawn. They had just six days

[24] *2 Corinthians 4:7 (Amplified Bible)*
[25] *Thoughts from Romans 8*

to do a quick visit. As the time was so short they recorded as much as they could and left a playback recorder so that the Paumarí could continue to listen to the word of God. There was a growing interest and understanding of the scriptures and it would be heartbreaking to see their work come to a complete standstill. They did not know what to expect or whether they would even be allowed to stay in Brazil.

As the restrictions continued, the members could only cry out to God for a miracle. They were hurting and perplexed. Brazil was their adopted country and the village people were like their own family now. It would be the indigenous groups who would suffer the most. For many, their only contact with the outside world was with the people who had chosen to come and live with them. They had little other medical help, but the government position remained unchanged.

As Shirley prayed and cried through some of the frustrations, many thoughts came to her about valleys. She read again the words from Psalm 84:

"Blessed (happy, fortunate, to be envied) is the man whose strength is in You, in whose heart are the highways to Zion. Passing through the Valley of Weeping (Baca), they make it a place of springs; the early rain also fills (the pools) with blessings. They go from strength to strength (increasing in victorious power); each of them appears before God in Zion."[26]

Was the Psalmist really declaring that the person who went through the Valley of Weeping was someone to be envied? He seemed to say that in going through it, they would then come out of it with a strength which they had not known before, and even then go on from strength to strength. As Shirley pondered the truth of the Psalm, she mused on the fact that valleys in our lives were not a sign of failure or sin, although there was no doubt that God could certainly use them to challenge us if He needed to catch our attention on some issue.

[26] *Psalm 84: 5-7 (Amplified Bible)*

How easy it was to try and take a detour around the valley and get past it as quickly as possible. The more she thought about it, the more it seemed as though our heart attitude in the valley was vital. The promise about valleys all seemed to point to a process of going through the valley and, far from losing strength there, to come out at the other end, stronger, more mature and anticipating victory in our lives and circumstances.

They had walked through the valley of the shadow of death many times. There had been frustrations and disappointments. Even now, the future was very uncertain. There were questions about suffering and sickness which had no easy answers. But through it all, God had never left them. He had been their strength. He had provided for them time and time again. There was no need to fear evil.

Shirley thought again about Psalm 23 and was reminded of the truth that God is the good shepherd, taking them through the valleys. He was the one who had guided them, been with them, and kept them all the way. If there were more valleys to come then they would not try to claw their way out, but would allow God to take them through, confident that He was working out some far bigger plan. He always had their good at heart.

12 New life

Meinke was back from convalescence long before the government decided on their policy regarding the ongoing work among the indigenous groups. During that seemingly endless and frustrating time of waiting for official news, Shirley and Meinke were themselves occasionally granted special permission by their local official to go to the village for a day or two. They felt that in many ways it was less to respect what they were doing and more to get information which he himself needed to do his own job, but the reasons did not matter too much so long as they were allowed to go. It was all a bit unpredictable and, like the unresolved lawsuit, the situation rumbled on. In fact it was to be seven long and very frustrating years before restrictions were fully lifted. In the meantime, they continued translation work as best they could.

Although the door of opportunity into the villages had been closed for such a long time, eventually it began to creak open once more. During the years when there had been so little access, some ground had been lost in terms of literacy, health and belief. It took a while to get things back to where they were.

Although daily life was never boring, living with creepy crawlies was always tedious. Several types of ants got into everything. A new kind of cockroach arrived and had a particularly nasty smell. They multiplied at a phenomenal rate and thrived on the insecticide, DDT. Scorpions and centipedes hid in wet towels and presented a significant danger. Army ants often marched through the house. Snakes would look in through the screens and it needed constant vigilance to watch out for the poisonous ones.

In the early hours of one morning Shirley made her way back through the darkened village after delivering a baby. She was exhausted. As she prepared to climb under her mosquito net, she heard a rustling noise and to her horror, found that a mouse was already there. It had been startled by her presence and was desperately trying to escape. She had no desire to share her sleeping space with a mouse and grabbed at it from outside the net. She was successful in catching it and held on tight, not quite sure what to do next. Before long the tiny form stopped struggling. Whether it died of fright or asphyxia was never decided.

Later on, another mouse also took up residence. It had a voracious appetite and each night worked its way through toilet paper, shoes and clothing. It was incredible how much a tiny creature could consume. War was declared. Shirley was armed with torch in one hand and machete in the other. The mouse won!

A different tactic was needed and they decided to have a cat. Although it was still a young kitten, the mouse took the hint and moved out. By now, however, bats had become a problem. They took up residence in the roof and their droppings were a real nuisance. Shirley was getting desperate with the problem and added it to her list of prayers. The answer came in an unexpected way.

All the dogs in the village got rabies and died. No human was bitten but it was still a very scary time. The bats then began to disappear too, and it seemed as though they were the ones who had brought the infection into the village. The kitten began to act strangely and also died.

Termites were a menace. Together with other insects they fed constantly on the wood and palm roof, and it was almost impossible to launch a successful counter attack. As a result, the life of a house was only about two years. So when a large lizard took up residence, Shirley and Meinke were more than happy to welcome it to their home as it lived on insects which devoured the house. But the budding friendship came to a swift conclusion.

The rabies crisis was long past and a colleague sent them – via the plane – a large and very beautiful white cat. Her husband's asthma was making it impossible for them to keep it. The cat had barely set paw into the house when the unsuspecting lizard became her first meal. Their shopping lists had not included cat food and later that day they wondered what else to feed her. Perhaps a tin of sardines might go down rather well. She took one look at the plate and left the house in some disgust. Moments later she was back with another lizard in her mouth which she seemed to relish. She made it clear that she was perfectly capable of looking after herself.

Medical crises continued to happen all the time. A young teenage girl had a very difficult breech delivery and Shirley's midwifery skills and experience were stretched to the limit. Amazingly, both mother and baby survived. Previously rather rebellious, the mother decided to turn her life over to Jesus and also dedicated the future of her baby to God's care.

One day Shirley got called to a nearby house where a lady had just delivered a baby boy. All had appeared to go well, but the placenta had not appeared. As Shirley examined the mother she got a shock. There was a second baby which was still to be delivered! Twins were a rare phenomenon amongst the Paumarí and in some traditions they were regarded with deep suspicion. Shirley wondered how the mother would react to the news.

Although shocked, the mother was happy enough at the prospect of having twins, but there was still a problem. The second baby was a breech presentation and Shirley wondered if all would indeed be well. To her immense relief, a little sister was safely born soon afterwards. Both babies were a good size.

The drama, however, was not quite over. Shirley took a sterile blade to cut the little girl's umbilical cord. Just at that moment the baby suddenly moved her leg and it got caught on the edge of the razor. It was a bit ironic to assist with the delivery of twins only to cut the baby's leg within moments of it being born. It was not quite according to the book. Fortunately it was not a deep cut and all was well. The babies thrived.

There was great excitement at the arrival of Dr Glenda, a Brazilian paediatrician, who came to work with the Dutch mission. The proposed site for their project was about a three-hour canoe trip away but there were endless delays in getting it started. In the meantime, Glenda came to live in the village and shared Shirley and Meinke's home. Oh the bliss of having help with the medical work.

Fátima was a regular language helper but at seven months pregnant, she suddenly developed severe toxaemia. Her response to medication was poor and supplies were low. Her life was in grave danger. Shirley, Meinke and Glenda paused to pray. Without more advanced facilities, it was looking grim. Soon after that she went into labour, but sadly the baby was stillborn. Fátima, however, was alive and made a full recovery.

News about the lawsuit was scant, although there were rumours of bribery but no one was really sure. In the end it simply fizzled out.

The population of the village was slowly beginning to grow and additional houses were built to accommodate the number of families. New villages were also emerging on non-flood ground and the bank of the river. Shirley and Meinke's own house was now vastly improved from the 10ft square floor and roof structure which had been home when Shirley had first arrived. The asbestos roofing allowed rain water to drain into a water butt and that helped with the question of drinking water.

Although the days were already full to bursting, Shirley had not forgotten the Paumarí who were living on the Tapauá River, and there remained within her a longing to help them in some way. Their needs were so great and it was hard to know where to begin. To do nothing, however, did not seem to be an option and so Shirley and Meinke began to make plans for a visit.

Shirley had vivid memories of the survey trip which she had done with Mary Ann and they were under no illusions about the challenge before them now as they stepped into the plane for the flight.

The pilot helped them unload their luggage, and left almost immediately. The same sense of isolation swept over them as the plane once more disappeared over the tree tops. They were reassured, however, that they had the radio and could call for help if it all got too much.

Reality hit hard and fast. The house and school which they had requested for the literacy course had not been built, so they decided to start on it themselves until help arrived. There were no outside walls and just a single, palm leaf screen which separated the living area from the rest. The roof was not water tight and although they had a piece of plastic, it was only big enough to cover one of the mosquito nets at night. The wind scattered their papers in all directions and the rain was a constant problem. Before long, the middle of the house began to slope dramatically, and it was only then that they realised it had been built over an ant's nest, deep in the ground. Lack of sleep caused frayed tempers.

In these difficult and stressful circumstances, it was the last straw to discover that once again, the two-way radio did not work. Had it done so, they would have been tempted to call for the pilot to come and get them. But they had no choice. They had come prepared to stay for three months and morale hit an all-time low. There was no escape.

To compound their misery, the young people made it clear that they did not want classes in Paumarí but only in Portuguese. But Shirley and Meinke had come with materials in Paumarí, and it was a struggle to produce enough lessons in Portuguese at such short notice. In desperation, Meinke asked one of the Paumarí if he could get her a rat to draw to help in her lesson. He went off willingly and quickly returned with a small, limp body. As he handed it to her, he asked if he could have it back at the end of the lesson so that it could be used for his supper.

Shirley and Meinke normally had an excellent friendship and working relationship, but the stress and strain of daily living caused cracks to appear. The power of witchcraft was particularly strong over the village and was clearly having a bad effect on them. Drunkenness in the village was rife.

As they took a walk together in the jungle one Sunday afternoon they stopped to look at a mass of tangled vines and both began to see an illustration of their present relationship. They determined to put things right.

As the days went past, they began to establish the custom of reading scripture aloud in the evenings as they did in their home village of Maraha. Mark's gospel was the first book to be read and the people listened intently. It was awesome to see the effect it had on them. There was no doubt that the word of God was alive and active. The people heard the truth of the gospel and they responded. Some of them decided that they wanted to be baptised. Like most other things in the village, even this was not without complications. The river was so fast flowing that the Paumarí leaders found it was impossible to pull the person back up once they had been immersed! The only option was to let them go, and for them to swim to shore.

There were two very weary ladies who later stepped into the float plane, but they now had a sense of excitement and some satisfaction. A small church had begun and they would never have seen it happen if they had escaped early on. There was so much more to do among the people, but it had been a start.

The Paumarí translation of the book of Acts was received back for final proofing. Galatians and Genesis were going through the printing process. Work continued on the gospel of Luke. Language helpers continued to ask searching questions. The Christmas story provided many of these.

Meinke was translating the gospel of Luke with Bitxi, her language helper. When she had finished reading the story to her,[27] Bitxi looked distressed.

"Why didn't Mary want the baby?" she asked anxiously.

Meinke was surprised at the question. "What makes you think that she didn't want him?"

"Well, as soon as the baby was born Mary laid him down. That is terrible. We would never put a baby down at all. How could she do that?" Bitxi continued to look distressed. "And to put the baby in the animal's feeding trough. Was she giving him to the animals to eat?"

As Meinke considered the story from a Paumarí perspective, she began to understand Bitxi's anguish. Other language helpers were shocked that Mary and Joseph were refused hospitality, especially as they were in such desperate need of shelter. In their culture, that was nothing short of sin.

A young couple came to see Shirley. They were understandably nervous. Their unborn baby was due to arrive shortly, but three previous children had all died before they had reached the stage of walking. They had taken the children to the shaman and done all the good things a parent was expected to do. The shaman had done all the things which he thought was right to do. But the children had still died.

Baiharo and his wife Oko wanted this child to be dedicated to God. They had heard a little of the Bible stories from Shirley and Meinke, but had not yet decided that they themselves would embrace this new faith system which was being

[27] *Luke 2 – no specific translation*

presented to them. However, they were desperate to have a healthy baby and perhaps felt that they had nothing to lose. Shirley and Meinke prayed with them, and once their baby daughter was born, the new parents put the life of Maria Lora into Jesus' hands. They had listened to the story of mothers bringing their children to Jesus for Him to bless them, and wanted to do the same.

A few other parents cautiously began to question whether the rituals of the shaman were the best for their child. Some decided that they would follow the teachings of Jesus. Others tried to do both. It was a huge decision for them, but it needed a gradual exposure to the power of God's word. There was no middle road. It was light or darkness. However, a tiny church had begun.

Most of the regular residents of the Maraha village had been listening fairly regularly to the translated scriptures. Although many of them would have said that they believed in Jesus, their children were still being taken to the night time rituals. The step between head belief and heart trust had not yet been taken.

Shirley and Meinke felt that the Lord was telling them to focus on His story of the two roads; the one broad road that leads to destruction and the other narrow road that leads to life. It is impossible to walk on both. A decision was needed. They could not obey the shaman and Jesus at the same time. They could not serve two masters. But could they trust themselves and their children into the hands of Jesus?

The shamans said that the children would die if the parents stopped appeasing the spirits. It was a time of intense inner struggle, but as one and another made their decisions, others soon began to follow. No appeal was made. They had to decide for themselves. Many came as families. It was always a privilege for Shirley and Meinke to pray for these new followers of Jesus. News spread that the shamans were seeing a shining light over the Maraha village at night, while everywhere else was in darkness.

All of the new followers of Jesus had been taken to the rituals as babies, and had participated in those held for their own children. Shirley and Meinke considered the forces at work in these new believers, and together with Paumarí they decided to hold a special service. It would give the villagers an opportunity to take themselves out of the influence of the spirits, and place themselves and their children into the hands of Jesus. It was a quiet but very powerful time as these transactions were made.

The next day it became clear that two shamans had been in the village the previous evening. They had begun to ask what was happening in Shirley's house. They had seen what looked like flames coming down on it, and yet it did not catch fire.

A spiritual fire had been lit, however, in the hearts of the people. Those who had been addicted to cigarettes and alcohol were completely set free. There were others who had not spoken to each other for years but now they were reconciled. They themselves asked to be baptised, so a service was organised to take place on the beach.

There was no mistaking the joy on their faces as they said how light they felt inside. It was clear that a huge weight of sin, fear and guilt had dropped off them. A shaman-in-training was one of those who decided to follow the teachings of Jesus. He testified that all his occult power disappeared when he was baptised.

The other shamans were not happy with these events and warned those who had not been baptised to stay away from them.

"Don't go into their houses. Don't eat their food," they warned. It seemed as though they thought 'it' could be caught, like the measles.

For some, there was real persecution. One young man was told that he was no longer welcome at home. It was a big thing for him in a community which was so bound to family structures. Some had their crops destroyed.

The numbers attending the evening sessions of scripture reading remained good, and it was particularly exciting to hear some of the men read it for themselves. Slowly the numbers of people responding to the Christian faith were growing. It was a huge challenge for them to reject so much of what they had been taught by the shaman and to embrace a new faith and understanding, and it was not surprising that some struggled along the way, particularly when some of their neighbours treated them with derision. But the truth and power of God's word was becoming evident in people's lives, and others could not fail to be challenged.

One special day dawned bright and clear and there was an atmosphere of real excitement and anticipation. A flotilla of packed canoes set out to a sandy beach. Several of the Paumari had asked to be baptised and to publicly declare that they were now followers of Jesus. It was an exciting service and the first baptism for the Paumari on the Purus River. Some 23 people stood and declared to the onlookers that their old life with its sin and trust in spirits was now finished, and a new life of commitment and obedience to Jesus was just beginning. Back in the village they shared together in a communion service.

Shirley often heard God speak to her through the everyday things that went on around them. Thousands of ants, clinging together like tennis balls were often swept along by the current when the water was high. Individually, they would not have stood a chance. Together they had mutual support and protection. As soon as they found a suitable tree or the leg of a house, they would undo themselves and climb up to establish a new nest.

If a canoe lost its rudder it was impossible to steer a straight course. It was such a small piece of wood but so important.

From these examples Shirley was able to remind the Paumarí of the importance of staying together in unity of heart and mind, and the dangers of neglecting the truth of God's word. One or two of the men had lost their spiritual rudder for a while, but restoration made them stronger and more mature. They needed patience and understanding while they found their way.

One day Baiharo came running to Shirley.

"The baby is sick. My baby is sick." His cries were heartbreaking. "The baby is sick, just like the others were." Shirley's heart sank. Amazingly, Dr Glenda was visiting the village and worked hard on the baby, but it was deteriorating rapidly. Shirley left the baby with the doctor and called together the small group of new Christians to pray.

They had already devised a system amongst themselves that when they met together for prayer, each one was expected to take part in a designated order. Baiharo joined the group and he was last in line. The others poured out their hearts to God in anguish for the life of the baby, but when it came to Baiharo's turn to pray, he quietly and with great dignity did no more than thank the Lord for hearing their prayers. By the next morning the baby was significantly better and went on to make a full recovery.

It became clear that there was a real spiritual battle going on between the forces of good and evil surrounding the faith of these new believers and the work of the shamans. Three children who had been dedicated to the Lord were taken back to the shaman by their mothers, and all three subsequently died. One shaman even came to the point of saying,

"If a child has been dedicated to God, then do not bring it to me."

Job's experiences seemed especially poignant to Shirley, Meinke and the Paumarí themselves. Life seemed to be very challenging in so many ways. Shirley felt herself drawn to re-read the book of Job over again, and her mind began to think of ways in which she might translate it for the Paumarí. Like every other book they tackled it seemed at first to be an impossible task, but the only way was to make a start and see how it went.

Poor Job. So many questions. So much grief. Not only had he lost all his worldly wealth in terms of his vast stock of animals, but worse than that, far worse than anything, was the death of not one, not two but all ten of his children. A tragic accident had struck the house in which they were having a party, and all had died in the same night. It was too terrible to comprehend.

In the early chapters there was an unusual opportunity to eavesdrop on a conversation between God and Satan. They had discussed Job and his blameless character. But not only did God give Satan permission to test him, it seemed as though He had actually pointed Job out to Satan. Surely God would not goad him into singling Job out for the worst that Satan could do to him?

As Shirley set to work, she decided to do a straight translation of the beginning and the end of the book. The central chapters of Job's conversations with his three friends brought a lot of reflection. They had started out so well, as they sat with him in silent grief, but then followed the accusations and hypotheses. Shirley decided that she would do these, and Job's questions to God Himself, as a précis in story form. It proved to be a work which the Paumarí took to heart and was quoted by them for years to come.

Totoi and Gilsa had experienced sadness. Their only child had died while still a baby and Gilsa had been almost paralysed with grief. She had become so thin that she could hardly walk and many people feared that she might even die of a broken heart. Two years later they both decided to follow the truths which were being presented to them in the word of God. They took the step of faith in being baptised. Now, a few months after the baby's death there was a huge change in both of them. A deep joy seemed to flow out from them and they were able to sing again. Totoi became a regular language helper.

Gilsa had another baby who became critically ill. Shirley and Meinke were not in the village at the time, so Totoi and Gilsa set out for Lábrea to try and find some medical help. As they travelled downriver they met Shirley and Meinke who were on their way to the village, and decided to turn round and come back with them. The child hovered between life and death.

Shirley and Meinke did not know at that stage that the baby had been taken to a shaman. It was his grandfather. The believers gathered to pray. Shirley did all she could, but the baby died. It was a huge test of faith for everyone.

In the Paumarí culture, funerals were intensely private occasions. When a person died they would be laid out in the house for a few hours and people would gather round and wail. They might also express their opinions on the cause of death or what they had thought about the dead person. Burials had to take place within 24 hours.

Bodies had originally been buried upright. The jungle floor grew with such a speed that the graves were soon sealed in naturally to protect them from the rising waters. Silt added an extra layer of deposit. They had gradually begun to use the wood of old canoes to make coffins, and to lay the body horizontally. If there was no canoe available, then sometimes planks of wood left over from an old house would be improvised.

When Shirley had first arrived in the village it would only be the father who took a child for burial. It was hard to imagine the loneliness of grief as he dug a grave and buried his child with no one to help or comfort him. If it was an adult who was to be buried, then only the number of people needed to carry the body would attend. Even that tradition was now changing and it was touching to see another believer offer to go with Totoi to bury his baby.

Amazingly, Gilsa did not go to pieces. There was no doubt that she was grieving deeply for her child, but there was something different about her. There was a dignity and hope which emanated from her too. It took time, as it would for any mother in her situation, but as she worked through a natural grief process she was able to sing again, she was at peace and was even able to help another mother to care for her baby. It was proof to everyone that God was the God of all comfort, and that He could bring hope out of despair when all human reasoning had failed. Perhaps it was a supernatural touch like this which Job had experienced when he could declare, "Naked I came from my mother's womb, and naked I will depart. The LORD gave and the LORD has taken away; may the name of the LORD be praised".[28]

[28] *Job 1:21 (NIV ©1984)*

The rat used in class and then for supper

13 Amazing help

Literacy classes for the men had been tried several times before. They had not been entirely successful, although some of the women were doing quite well. The men had so many interruptions and were often out fishing, collecting nuts, lumber or rubber. Shirley and Meinke decided that they would have one more attempt at organising another class, but that this time it would have strict rules. There would be standards to attain and if the men missed a certain number of lessons, they would be out. They wondered how this kind of approach would be received but, to their surprise, there was real enthusiasm.

"Oh, it's a real school now if it has rules!" The men built what was in reality just a shack, but to them it was their school. They also made some benches and chairs, although the quality left a lot to be desired and most collapsed in a very short time. However, the idea was good and the term began. It was high water season and some of the children took their fathers to school by canoe so that they could take it back for the family to use. Sometimes a class was interrupted by the sight of a large fish swimming beneath them. Once it was speared the class could continue.

One day during classes a local trader came into the village and demanded to take the men away on a trip. He declared that they were all in debt to him and that they needed to do what he said. He was very threatening in his manner and made it clear he had a gun.

Shirley and Meinke wondered how to handle this situation. It was very tense. They went into the kitchen to pray. Even as they did so, they heard the sound of the float plane, the 'Lake Amphibian'. It was totally unexpected. The highly charged atmosphere in the school room was defused by the sound of the plane and all of them gathered at the edge of the lake to see who had come. To their surprise, a representative of FUNAI stepped out, and with him was the FUNAI lawyer. Some time earlier Shirley and Meinke had met a General in Porto Velho. On that occasion he had made the passing comment that if they ever needed his help, they only had to ask. Now here was the help right in the village, at just the right moment.

They discovered that the lawyer was in the process of preparing a court case. It was known that this local trader sold alcohol to the Paumarí and other indigenous groups, and this was illegal. Their arrival could not have come at a better time. They took the man who had been threatening the Paumarí to one side and gave him a real dressing down. When he told them that he was owed money they said,

"Write the debts down and tie them to the tail of a deer. Then try to catch it." In other words, "Write it off!"

They made it very clear to him that he was the one in trouble, not the Paumarí. Shirley and Meinke were so grateful that God had heard their cry for help long before they had uttered it, when the plane was already on the way. The situation could have turned very nasty but the whole thing had been turned around. She was later able to use it as a means of describing the legal and justice systems, and the powers of the police. Since the Paumarí had no concept of such things, it had been hard to describe what it meant to have debts cleared and an advocate acting on their behalf. It had been a powerful moment for Shirley and Meinke personally to be reminded that "Before they call, I will answer; while they are still speaking I will hear".[29] They were able to share this illustration with the Paumarí too.

As another Christmas approached, there was huge rejoicing with Totoi and Gilsa over the birth of a healthy baby

[29] *Isaiah 65:24 (NIV ©1984)*

daughter. Shirley, Meinke and the Paumarí made plans for a Christmas presentation. On Christmas Eve everyone squeezed together while the wonderful story was read aloud and the children acted out the parts. It had become a tradition that a new mother and her baby would take the part of Mary and Jesus. This year Gilsa, Totoi and their new baby took the central roles. What a relief to Shirley and Meinke that the previous misunderstandings about the Christmas story had been resolved, and that it was presented as a cause for great celebration.

As a new year began, Totoi came one morning to ask if he could be relieved of leading the service that day, as he needed to go to another village where his father was sick. This was a surprising victory. Reliability was not a feature of the Paumarí, and to have someone come and explain that they could not do something and give a reason why, was a real breakthrough. In general, they would just not turn up. Later in the day he was back again. He had no peace about his decision not to lead the meeting, and said that he would do it after all. It was a double victory indeed.

The float plane had been sold, and since that time travel to and from the village had become much more difficult. The Lake Amphibian had been replaced with a Cessna on wheels, but that did not help in the villages where there was no airstrip. Some teams were constructing a suitable runway, but because the ownership of the land where the Paumarí lived was still in dispute, it was felt unwise to do the same.

For several years, Shirley and Meinke either took a commercial flight or JAARS plane from Porto Velho to the town of Lábrea. From there it was necessary to hire a canoe with outboard motor, but that could involve a wait of many days. Once the journey had begun the volume of luggage made it a slow trip and they often had to stay overnight at a riverside dwelling. On leaving the village the tedious trip was done in reverse.

From time to time the new wheel plane had occasion to pass near Lake Maraha, and the pilot used to drop a package of mail for Shirley and Meinke. The strip of land between the lake and houses was quite narrow, so it was not an easy manoeuvre. One such drop from the plane hit the bedroom roof and shattered some of the asbestos sheets. On a more sophisticated drop, the pilot attached the parcel to a small parachute. It was a good idea in theory. However, it landed high up in a nearby tree and there was much excitement as the men tried to coax it down.

One day the sound of the plane overhead was a surprise. They were not expecting it. Along with the villagers they looked up to see what was happening. As it circled round, a hand reached out and dropped a parcel. It had a white bandage around it to help them find it. More mail! How exciting.

One of the letters came as a bit of a shock. Four young Brazilians from a group called 'Youth With a Mission' were coming to work with the Paumarí on the Tapauá River, and wanted to stay with Shirley and Meinke for a month to learn all they could. They would be arriving soon. Four of them! Where would they put them? How would they feed them? How would the 'toilet' cope? What if the ground flooded as it often did at that time of the year? Later in the day Shirley watched silently as Meinke stood at the water's edge and, like King Canute, forbade it to come any closer! It did not.

Somehow everything came together. The young people, two of whom were newly married, fitted in extremely well. They brought some supplies with them and were willing to take their share of the chores. They were full of enthusiasm and their visit brought real friendship and delights.

When an airstrip was ready in an Apurina village, travel arrangements improved to some degree although it was still not easy. Once they had landed, they had to walk for a while, then take a canoe, walk a bit further, take another canoe, walk again and take yet another canoe. By previous arrangement they hoped that some of the Paumarí would be waiting to help them with the luggage for the final part of the journey back to Maraha.

There was eager anticipation when FUNAI decided that the Paumarí needed their own airstrip. There were not many suitable places as the ground either flooded completely or was waterlogged in the wet season. However, one piece of land did seem as though it might be a possibility. It was a mammoth task. Once the trees had been felled, they had to clear the ground and remove the enormous roots which were hidden below the surface. If the plane hit a hidden tree stump, the result could be disastrous. Although the Paumarí men got involved in the project, they needed outside help. A team came from Porto Velho, and some Americans who were on short-term assignment also arrived. They brought some useful equipment which proved invaluable. The airstrip was the focal point in what became the village of Crispinho.

The Paumarí had traditionally planted on the wide, sandy beaches at the side of the Purus River. Manioc, water melon and sweet corn were their main crops. As time went by an increasing number of non-indigenous people took up residence along the river, mainly as workers for the land owners, to tap the rubber trees.

The Paumarí started to make fields from what had been virgin jungle. It was an immense task to fell the trees using an axe and there was no adequate way to clear the ground for planting except to wait for all the chopped undergrowth to dry in the hot sun and then burn it. This always presented a danger to the houses and sometimes the fire would rage out of control, destroying a neighbour's field in the process. Tempers could burn as hot as the fire. Whilst they were highly skilled in fishing which seemed to come naturally to them, farming was a burdensome necessity.

Being, as they were, semi-nomadic fishermen, they often moved at various times during the year, either to be near their crops to protect them from thieves, or to fish at certain locations when it was known the fish would appear.

It was rare for many days to pass without some medical crisis. Zaíra was a very sick toddler. She had been suffering from malaria but her mother had neglected to give her the treatment. Now she lay unconscious. Two of the shamans walked by the house and looked in. They knew from experience that a child who was so sick did not have long to live. No one asked them for their help so they just watched silently to see what would happen.

Rasi, the child's mother was desperate. She had asked the Christians to come and pray. Shirley and Meinke joined them, although their faith was feeling a bit weak. They all prayed and asked for God's mercy. There seemed to be no change in the child.

Zaíra's father was seen going around the village with a small bottle, and asking other mothers to provide some breast milk which he could give his daughter. Someone waved raw fish over her face, but not surprisingly, she did not react. Shirley and Meinke were still in the house when Fátima arrived back in the village. She had been away on a trip for several days and had only just returned and heard the news. She picked her way through the legs of people sitting on the floor and gathered up Zaíra from her mother's lap. The toddler remained limp and motionless.

Fátima began to walk around with Zaíra in her arms. She reminded the Lord of all the miracles which she had heard about from the scriptures. Then she thanked Him for every healing which had happened within their village. She prayed on at some length, affirming her confidence in God that He would do the same for Zaíra. With nothing left to be said, she placed the unconscious form back in her mother's arms and everyone left the house. By the next morning, Zaíra was up and about, eating normally and well on the road to recovery! God had done it again.

Others were also being challenged or encouraged. "I was feeling discouraged and did not want to follow Jesus anymore. Then I started to read God's word and I became happy again."

"After my husband left me people kept telling me to go after other men in order to get some money. God's word said I should not do that and I want to do what God says."

"We were looking for Mara and the children who were lost in the flooded jungle. It was dark and raining heavily. We could not hear or see them. I said that we should stop and pray because God knows where they are and can show us the way. We found them the same night."

Chico also gave testimony. "God is really powerful. I had borrowed Totoi's canoe but last night it floated off in the storm. I was so worried. I asked God to put it somewhere safe and this morning when I went to look for it, I found that it had been caught in some trees not far away." It was not uncommon for canoes to be lost in tropical storms.

Joâo Koro told us he had been collecting rubber latex in the jungle. Suddenly he became aware that a black panther was nearby and he hastily began to climb a slender tree. He managed to stay above the animal which was obviously considering him for lunch. The tree was too thin for the panther to climb so it remained below, waiting. Joâo Koro was getting tired of hanging on. He suddenly thought, "I should ask God to help me". He had not been praying for long when the panther simply walked away.

It was time for Shirley to have some more home leave, and once more it was a time of adjustment to culture and climate. She caught up with friends and visited some of her supporters. There were encouraging letters from the Paumarí. Baiharo had begun to be a pastor and many people seemed to be responding in a positive way to his leadership. Dosohani had been leading some services in another village. Several men had led the singing and reading of scripture. Others were waiting for some instruction on how to preach. The shaman was speaking out against them but in general, they were encouraging one another and standing firm in their faith. Shirley did some work on the book of Titus while she was in England. Time passed quickly and a large part of her heart was with the Paumarí.

Back in the village once more the work continued. Some days were routine, others were dramatic, many were challenging and all were busy. There seemed to be a lot of illness and with resistance low, several people seemed to get one thing after another. Flu, malaria and pneumonia were common.

Meinke's health continued to be up and very seriously down. Dangerously high fevers struck suddenly and without warning. It was eventually diagnosed that she had myalgic encephalomyelitis (ME). This devastating illness was poorly understood but could attack almost any organ of the body with varying degrees of intensity. It was chronic, debilitating and for Meinke, often life-threatening.

During 1985 Meinke had needed thyroid surgery. The doctor had not wanted her to stay in hospital a moment longer than was absolutely necessary as he was concerned about her getting some infection, so she was discharged the day after the operation. She was under the care of a doctor in Porto Velho, but three months after the surgery she was diagnosed with hepatitis B. Recovery was slow, but eventually she seemed well enough to travel. Plans were made for them to go together to southern Brazil to see some of Meinke's family and to visit their mutual supporters.

As Christmas approached Meinke was very poorly. The hepatitis had caused the serious complication of cirrhosis of the liver and, as a result of that, she had been suffering from severe haemorrhages. They both knew that these were an extremely serious marker of the end stage. After discussions with their leadership, they decided to return to the village for Christmas as planned. The radio system to Porto Velho now had an emergency button and Shirley knew that she could call the centre for help at any time.

FUNAI had given them a lot of vaccines to take with them for the Paumarí. By now Meinke had trained some health workers in the village who were quite capable of giving injections.

Even as they left Meinke was experiencing some breathing problems and a bit of chest pain, but never one to make a fuss, she assumed that it was probably related to one of her existing conditions. Once in the village, Shirley kept one eye on the vaccination programme and another on Meinke. When they had finished their work, they gathered to pray for Meinke. She was extremely weak and had developed a high fever.

It slowly dawned on Shirley that this could be polio. It was a terrifying prospect, not just for Meinke but for the whole village. She asked God for a sign. If the breathing problems continued, then they would leave as soon as possible. But by morning Meinke's breathing was significantly better.

Their pilot, Don, his wife and three children came to stay just before Christmas. Meinke's condition fluctuated and she had another haemorrhage. She was barely conscious. Don wanted to take Meinke out the following morning, but strange as it seemed, Shirley could get no peace about this although it was the obvious thing to do. Once more she prayed for a sign, and once more God answered. By morning Meinke could walk and some of the other symptoms had improved, although the liver problem remained. At this stage, polio seemed an unlikely diagnosis.

As New Year's Day dawned Meinke deteriorated, and by lunchtime she was in a deep coma. As Shirley called the Paumarí believers to join her she knew that once more, Meinke's life hung in the balance. She was having frequent convulsions. Some of the unbelievers began to prepare for a burial.

The Christian believers continued to pray. After about five hours, Meinke suddenly sat up! She was confused as to why there were people in her bedroom. Shirley gently explained to her that she had been unconscious and on the brink of death.

Meinke then shared what had happened to her. She had been aware of an experience of going somewhere, and it had taken her to the presence of Jesus.

She said "I got to a place where everything was beautiful. The further I went the more wonderful it became. There was peace all around me. I felt weightless and all the burdens of this life had fallen off. I was dancing in all this beauty. I felt that all the light, joy and peace emanated from Jesus. There are just no words to describe it all".

It was a profound experience for them all. There was no doubt that she had come back from the brink of death. But even so, health issues remained. Some things were healed. Others were not. There were no answers.

As soon as she was able, Meinke went back to work. She continued working on a translation of Luke's gospel while Shirley tackled Colossians. Once she had finished Luke, Meinke set to work on Matthew. Later on Baiharo brought his family out to Porto Velho to check it with them.

Four of those who had trained in literacy taught some of the children to read and that proved a great success. They gave five half days a week for eleven weeks with no pay. However, they did not feel they could continue indefinitely without some remuneration, and it was hard to know where it might come from. If payment was given from outside, the project would stop if the financial support dried up. It would be much better if it could be self supporting in some way. They tried to get the parents to pay either with farinha or paraffin, but this did not prove very satisfactory.

In 1989 Rodolfo Senn, an Argentinean, and his Swiss wife, Beatrice, came with their children to help Shirley and Meinke with their work among the Paumarí. They were also members of SIL. They immediately got stuck into the business of learning the Paumarí language. Their plan was to take on what tasks they could so as to release Shirley and Meinke for translation. There was still a huge amount of work to be done before the New Testament could go for publication.

Beatrice took responsibility for the literacy classes, supervising and helping the teachers. She organised a regular meeting for the women. They shared some Bible teaching, but she also taught them sewing and embroidery. Rodolfo was able to give the men some new ideas about agriculture, which not only improved their food supply, but also helped economically. He built a small saw mill so that the men could utilise the trees which they had chopped down and use the wood for house building.

Rodolfo and Beatrice lived initially in Crispinho where the airstrip had been built. Plans were in hand for Shirley and Meinke to have a new house there. It was vastly superior to their previous village houses, and was to be built around a wooden frame. A short-term assignment team from Canada were helping with the house building, and Rodolfo, together with some of the men from Porto Velho, also got involved. It felt like a palace! The Senn family then moved into the empty house in Maraha, while the ladies enjoyed their new home.

Daily life was seldom without crises. Maria Macília was eight months pregnant when she had eclampsia. She was having convulsions. Shirley told her husband that he must get her to Lábrea immediately, but he took her to the shaman first and that resulted in a five hour delay. When they finally got her there to the little hospital, she had a C-section, but the baby was dead. She herself was unconscious for four days. As soon as she came round, the first thing she asked for was her book of Bible verses which she had been memorising. She and her husband recognised that it was God who had brought them through the crisis, and they both made the decision to put their lives in Jesus' hands.

Roni was in the final days of his life. He suffered from kleptomania, so was known for stealing. It was a common practice for the Paumarí to withhold food and drink from an elderly person who became ill. Roni was dying and his relatives in another village stopped giving him anything to eat so that he would die more quickly. He was grossly swollen and unable to care for himself. He was brought to the village and Fátima took it upon herself to care for his every need. It was intensely moving. Roni made his peace with God before he died, and his was the first Christian funeral.

"Shirley! Meinke!" It was a Wednesday evening and Shirley had just put out the light ready for bed. She struggled to find her torch as the call grew more insistent. "Shirley! Help!"

They threw on some clothes and went out to see who was calling. It was Sapihai. His ten year old son Ba'dana had just been bitten by a very poisonous snake. Sapihai was almost beside himself with terror.

Shirley and Meinke quickly followed him through the village to the house and were there within a matter of minutes. As soon as they saw Ba'dana, they knew that he was in big trouble. His foot had already swelled alarmingly and the boy was obviously in great pain. It was clear that he was already suffering from internal bleeding, and blood oozed from his mouth. He was dangerously ill.

Some of the villagers had seen the snake, and they did not need to be told that the boy's life was in real danger. The fear was palpable. Shirley and Meinke exchanged a brief glance. Both knew that there were no supplies of anti-venom in the village.

There was no hope of an emergency flight at that time of night, and by morning it might well be too late. Even so, they pressed the emergency button on the radio to ask that colleagues should pray. What else could they do? It would need a miracle if this boy was to survive.

The radio technician who received the call responded with some startling advice. He told them that it was possible to use an outboard motor to produce an electrical shock. If this was applied to the site of the bite, it would neutralise the venom. He reported that it had been used successfully in other places where there had been no medical help.

It sounded a very risky procedure, but what were their options? They could either try it, or watch the boy die. Was there anything to lose? Shirley and Meinke sent some of the men off to find an outboard motor and as they waited for them to return, they did their best to reassure Ba'dana.

Not surprisingly, the boy was terrified. He was well aware of the fear all around him; he was in intense pain, and it was so frightening for him to find blood in his mouth. He was almost paralysed with terror as they set up the equipment near his foot and began the treatment. The radio operator had advised them to give blasts of shock for three seconds every 5-10 minutes. Ba'dana screamed with pain and fear as Sapihai held his boy tightly.

Within an hour the pain had gone! The bleeding had stopped and although the boy was exhausted, he was clearly feeling better. When Shirley and Meinke felt that it was safe enough to leave the family, they returned home for what was left of the night. They were exhausted too.

By the next morning Ba'dana was up and about. There was still some swelling around his foot but other than that, he was fine.

In time his foot returned to normal and he suffered no lasting effects from his traumatic experience. There was no doubt that God had, once more, heard the cry of the helpless.

Others from the village had watched in silence as the treatment was applied, and they themselves began to use it successfully in many other cases.

Please do not try this at home!

Meinke teaching the men's literacy class

Totoi and Gilsa celebrate their new baby and act as Mary and Joseph in the Christmas presentation

14 Momentous moments

Way back in the early 1970s, Baiharo and Oko had been the first to dedicate their child, Maria Lora, to Jesus, rather than take her to the shaman for the rituals. Their step of faith had led the way for others to do the same, and the early Paumarí church had been born as a result. That little baby girl was now a teenager who had made her own decision to follow the teaching of Jesus.

Shirley and Meinke never made appeals to the Paumarí. They did not want declarations to be made on the basis of pleasing them. It had to be a personal decision. Every baptism was special, as one by one the villagers were making the choice to declare their new faith publicly before their friends and family. One baptism was particularly poignant. It was Maria Lora.

One and another of the Paumarí also made life-changing decisions. Edilson had longed to study ever since he was 16 years old. Now that he was in his twenties, he begged Shirley and Meinke to help him make his dream come true. They were due to be leaving the village the very next day and, knowing that this was not just some passing flight of fancy, agreed to see what could be done. His face was a picture when they told him that they would try and get him enrolled at an Indigenous Bible College which was for many different ethnic groups. His course of study would be for three years, and it was no small undertaking.

He had long-term plans too. After graduation he wanted to complete his studies in Portuguese, but agreed to go back and help his own people for a year. Shirley and Meinke knew that anyone who left the security of their cultural environment would encounter many problems and misunderstandings along the way.

It had been a hard week. Shirley had been having some back trouble for a few days, and Meinke had run short of some of her medication. Both had been feeling a little under the weather, but there was great excitement at the proposed visit of two friends. One was from Shirley's home church in England, and the other an Austrian friend of Meinke's. It was a particularly hot day as they listened carefully for the sound of the plane, and as soon as it came within earshot they were out with many of the villagers to welcome these special guests, Kate and Edith. There were plenty of goodies in their visitor's luggage and there was so much to talk about.

The next day Shirley arranged with Antônio, one of the Paumarí men, to take them on a trip to see other Paumarí villages. Plans were meticulously made for them to see as much as possible of the local area. Antônio came over to ask if he could have a small quantity of petrol so that he could check out the engine of his outboard motor, in readiness for the trip.

It was a reasonable enough request so Shirley picked up the bottle and started to transfer some from their container into his. It was something which they never normally did in the house. Almost instantly the fumes from the petrol shot across the floor of the house to the pilot light on the gas fridge. With a whoosh the flames were high within seconds. There was a bottle of gas at the fridge and another on the stove. The gas within them ignited and it was as though two enormous blow torches were aimed at the walls.

"Get out! Everyone get out!" Meinke shouted.

As they scrambled out of the house the heat was chasing them. The speed at which it took hold was almost unbelievable. A number of the Paumarí rushed up to the house and a group of men immediately took decisive action. Beneath the house there were six full canisters of gas. Normally, these were chained one to another and around a leg of the house. For some unknown reason, although they were linked to each other that day, they were not attached to the house. Each one was incredibly heavy and there was no way that one person could have moved them all.

Shirley and Meinke watched in silent horror as the men dived in under the house. Flames were coming out of all the screened windows. What the men were doing would save an even greater disaster. The thought of six canisters exploding was terrifying. Who knows how many people might have been killed or seriously burnt? It was only as they emerged unscathed that Shirley realised she had been holding her breath.

As she let it out, there was nothing anyone could do except stand in shock and watch as the house burnt to the ground. The fire was totally out of control. When the flames finally died down, there was nothing left but charcoal and a few bits of twisted metal. Somewhat bizarrely, the back steps were still in one piece.

One of the Paumarí women clung to Shirley.

"We thought you were still in there," she sobbed, her gulps coming from deep within her. It was an unusual show of emotion. As Shirley did her best to comfort the lady, her own tears were not far away.

Everyone was safe, but *everything* had gone. Kate and Edith's luggage was burnt to a crisp and they did not even have their shoes on when they fled. All the language material was now a pile of ashes. Clothes, books, medical notes, stores... everything was destroyed. A blackened, twisted blob of something was probably the remains of the two-way radio. It was unrecognisable.

The Paumarí quickly responded to the disaster, and their concern, comfort and generosity was very moving. They offered clothes, mosquito nets and blankets. Food appeared along with room in a house for the ladies to sleep in that night. The following day Rodolfo was finally able to get a message to Porto Velho, and the pilot promised to come and collect them straight away. Kate and Edith's long awaited visit to the village resulted in just two nights there. It was very strange to possess absolutely nothing other than the clothes they stood in, but they were all grateful to be alive.

It was touching to hear some of the responses from the Paumarí.

"It is like the story of Job," observed Rasi. "He lost everything, but God gave it back to him and He will also take care of you."

"This is what it will be like when Jesus returns," commented Fátima. "There will be no time to do anything."

"Satan is trying to destroy the church, but he will not succeed because Jesus is stronger," commented Totoi. Lots of people stood silently watching.

Later that evening the followers of Jesus gathered together. They thanked God that they had all got out alive and sang a song of worship, based on the verses from the Psalms, "Bless the Lord, O my soul, Bless the Lord O my soul, and all that is within me, bless His holy name".[30]

All of the precious translation was backed up in Porto Velho on computer disk, although the most recent work was lost. Over the years Shirley had tried to keep family records of Paumarí births, marriages, deaths and other important dates. That information was lost forever. By this time, she had a computer in the village but together with all her other personal possessions, that was also destroyed. Education materials and scripture books would have to be replaced over time. Many items of school and health records and lesson plans were irreplaceable.

Back in Porto Velho Shirley and Meinke went to the Federal Police Office to notify them that some documents had been

[30] *"Bless the Lord, O my soul". Words: Anonymous. Based on verses from Psalm 103*

lost. The police officer asked them if they had called the
fire brigade!

In the days that followed, Meinke and Shirley marvelled at
the way God provided. They took a short break with Kate
and Edith to visit the stunning Iguaçu Falls on the border of
Brazil and Argentina. Rodolfo took the lead in organising and
implementing plans for a new house. Downriver at a saw mill
there was just the right amount of wood which was needed.
A second hand furniture store in Porto Velho had plenty of
stock and exactly what they required. Some months later
when they were in the vicinity again, it was almost empty.

The fire had occurred in April. By mid-August the new house
was complete. It was a remarkable achievement. It would
not have been surprising if the translation work had slowed
down as a result of the fire. In reality, the opposite was true.
Perhaps it was that many people had prayed for them during
that time.

Shirley herself was keeping a close watch on the size
and shape of her little finger. A benign tumour had been
removed on a visit to England a couple of years previously,
but now it seemed to be growing again. She made contact
with a doctor friend back in England who had arranged the
previous surgery for her, and awaited further instructions.

The surgeon's reply was that she should have further surgery
as soon as possible. If she waited until she was next due for
home leave, then it might mean that amputation was the
only option. It was strange to contemplate. This little digit
on the human body rarely got a mention, but now that
someone had talked of chopping it off, she suddenly felt
quite attached to it. They could not do that. It was an old
friend! She made plans for a short trip to England.

As she returned to the village after the surgery, she found
that there was great concern for Carlito. He had become

increasingly immobile, so she and Meinke eventually took him with them to Porto Velho for some medical checks. His wife Marilda and their three year old daughter Marisa came along too. His problem was eventually diagnosed as TB which had caused severe degeneration of two vertebrae. He was almost completely paralysed.

He was, understandably, quite depressed. He could hardly bear to think about a life-time of dependency on someone else, and in addition, Marilda's family were putting pressure on her to leave him and find a new husband who would not be such a burden. He was barely twenty at the time.

Within a few weeks of him starting treatment, there was some improvement. Shirley and Meinke had particularly asked their supporters to pray for Carlito. After taking part of the treatment he returned to the village to complete it there.

A few weeks later there was great excitement!

"Have you seen Carlito? He's starting to walk again!" The village was a-buzz with excitement. There he was, on his feet. It was not long before he could also go fishing. God had answered prayer once more.

There were other encouragements too. The first Christian wedding was one such cause for celebration. For the first time ever, a Paumarí lady, Zefinha, and a Paumarí man, Banti, stood before a Paumarí pastor, Baiharo, and made their wedding vows. None of them had ever seen a wedding before. Banti was the pastor of the tiny church on the Tapauá River which had been nurtured into existence by the group of young people who had come to visit earlier. Banti had made a visit to the village where Shirley and Meinke lived, and the moment he had seen Fátima's daughter, Zefinha, it had been love at first sight.

Until that time the Paumarí in general just started to live with one another in the girl's home. The mother could take her daughter away if the husband did not live up to her expectations. Now they were deciding to make promises to one another, "for as long as I live". This was something totally new. It was exciting that Zefinha was willing to wait for a suitable Christian husband. Lives were being changed in many ways.

Another crisis loomed. News reached them of a cholera epidemic upriver. This was extremely worrying and they listened anxiously for further updates. Before long, six of the Paumarí were ill and it was not hard to diagnose the problem. Cholera had reached their village. In a place which had no fresh running water, a contaminated supply was a real threat to the whole community, and Shirley and Meinke were under no illusions as to the seriousness of their situation. Those who were sick had severe diarrhoea, and adequate hygiene was hard to maintain. They gathered the health workers together and reminded them of the nature of the disease. Dehydration was a serious threat to life, so they taught the health workers how to set up a drip of intravenous fluids. If they themselves became ill it would be good to have others who could cope with this life-saving treatment.

Health authorities sent some chlorine to add to the water for drinking and cooking. Shirley urged the people that any water they used should be boiled or filtered and if possible, both. A sick man was brought to the village by canoe. He was very ill. Amazingly, the pilot came by on an unplanned visit and he was able to rig up a makeshift bed on the floor of the plane and take the man to Porto Velho. Swift diagnosis and treatment saved his life. The condition of the sick Paumarí remained a great concern. Early treatment would buy them time, but they also needed hospitalisation.

The government had provided a large canoe with powerful outboard motor for such medical cases, and had also made an allowance of fuel. João Koro was asked if he would take the first two patients to Lábrea. If all went well the journey downriver would take six hours at best, but the return back upriver could take up to twelve hours. The prospect of more trips was daunting. Who else might be ill by the time he returned? An atmosphere of fear hung over the village.

João Koro set out with the first two patients, but as they made their way downriver he became very afraid. What would happen if he caught cholera too? Who would care for his wife and children if they caught it while he was away? That night he had a dream in which a shining figure appeared and drew a line around João Koro's house. The person spoke to him and said that the cholera would not pass that line. From that moment on, no one else caught cholera! The epidemic stopped completely and the Paumarí who had been sick returned to the village in due course.

Significant dreams were not uncommon among the people. At one point Fátima became very concerned about her dead mother and the two babies which she herself had lost. She had a dream in which she saw her mother with the children, who were about the age they would have been had they lived. Fátima went forward to embrace them but heard her mother say: "You must not touch us now. We are very happy here and one day you will join us."

Fatima found the experience a great comfort to her.

Her own daughter Zefina also lost her first baby in childbirth, and grieved deeply. Someone gave her a pet monkey which became like a surrogate baby. When she became pregnant again, Shirley was most concerned that the monkey would be jealous of the baby, but in the end it died before the baby was born. Shirley and Meinke had not been around for the birth of the first baby but were planning to be present for the delivery of Zefina's second child. Unfortunately, she had miscalculated her dates.

They arrived back in the village thinking that they were in plenty of time, but were greeted with an urgent call as soon as they stepped off the plane. Zefina was in labour and there was a problem. They ran from the plane to their house to get the maternity box, and then ran the length of the airstrip and as far again to the home where Zefina was in labour. They were extremely hot and thirsty when they arrived at the house, but there was no time to rest. The baby was ready to be born, but there were no contractions. Shirley gave her a uterine stimulant and before long a live baby was delivered. Everyone breathed a sigh of relief.

While Shirley attended to Zefina, Fátima took the child to wash it. Zefina began to haemorrhage. Shirley quickly gave more injections but urgently needed a bowl in which to wash her hands so that she could retrieve the placenta, and then help to clean up the new mother. But there was only one bowl and the baby was currently being bathed in it. After some moments of confusion, order was restored. Neither Fátima nor Zefina realised just how close they had been to another catastrophe. Once the baby was clean and dry and safely in her mother's arms, Shirley and Meinke gratefully made their way back home. It had been a rather more eventful day than they had expected.

One by one the initial translation of each of the books of the New Testament was completed. There continued to be moments when the truth of God's word hit home with power and conviction. Rasi was helping one day with some Bible stories from 1 Samuel. She listened carefully to the story she was hearing for the very first time. God was angry with Eli because he did not correct his two sons, even though he knew they were doing wrong things.

"That is just like us," she said thoughtfully. "We often see our children doing wrong things and we don't correct them. I should have corrected my boy the other day when he was doing something wrong."

At other times it was exciting to see how the Paumarí understood what they were reading. Baiharo had been listening to the book of Revelation for the first time and had been following the story as we might read a detective story, waiting with bated breath for the next development. He wanted to know how history would end. What a relief when he got to chapter twenty and he heard that Satan was to be bound and put into a very deep hole. But then... as they worked on he exclaimed:

"Oh! No! Not again!" Baiharo was horrified. "Why did He have to let him out?"

It was exciting to have a shaman acting as language helper for the translation work. He was clearly very challenged by what he was reading, but his wife threatened to leave him if he became a Christian. There would certainly be a cost for him if he made that decision. Whenever Shirley and Meinke shared the truth of God's word with the Paumarí, they never minimised this reality. It was good to see some deep conversations going on between the language helpers when they stopped for a coffee break.

Each book had to go through a complete revision once the whole New Testament was finished. Terminology had to be regularised. There were computer checks for commas, full stops, quotation marks and other such grammar. There were questions about typesetting. As all these details came together, plans were made for Shirley and Meinke to go to Dallas to assist with the typesetting. Once that was done, the precious manuscripts were sent to South Korea for printing. This was paid for by the Bible League.

The Dedication

Thirty-two years! Yes. It had been thirty-two years since
Shirley had first arrived in the Paumarí village. Her dream had
always been of the day when she would be able to give the
Paumarí the complete New Testament in their own language.
What a challenge it had been. She remembered back to the
time when she had the impression of a 10,000 piece jigsaw
puzzle in her mind, and how it seemed an almost impossible
task. But slowly, piece by piece, understanding had come.
Analysis of the sound and grammar systems had been
like the border of the jigsaw, and then groups of words or
principles had grown in number. In recent years, as one book
after another was completed in first draft, then checked and
rechecked, the picture began to take shape.

It was now 1996 and with the New Testament having been
printed, a service of Dedication was planned for 24th April.
This in itself was no easy task. Around twenty to thirty people
planned to come from around the world. Local directors and
associates of Wycliffe would be joined by representatives
from Germany and Switzerland, friends from England,
a member from Papua New Guinea, and relatives from
southern Brazil.

Once these visitors had arrived in Brazil and found their way
to Porto Velho, detailed plans were drawn up to fly them
in by twos and threes to the village. Where would they
all sleep? What would they eat? How would they provide
enough drinking water? How would the infamous hole in
the ground cope?

As the weeks passed, Shirley and Meinke were a little
anxious. The centre piece of the whole dedication – the
precious box of books – was nowhere to be seen. The
printing had been done in South Korea and as far as they
knew, the shipment had got as far as Rio.

By 16th April things were getting tense. A radio message then assured them that two boxes had been released from Customs. All that was needed were arrangements to pick them up.

By 1.30pm the same day another message brought bad news. Their contact in Rio had called to make arrangements for collection. He asked for reassurance that the two boxes did indeed hold the Paumarí New Testament. He was assured that they did...but then there was a hesitation. Well, the official thought that they did, but he could not say for sure.

By 2pm there was more bad news. The boxes which had been released did not hold the Paumarí work at all. They certainly contained a precious translation, but not the Paumarí New Testament.

By 2.45pm another call reported that the official would do all he could, but there was a two day strike planned. They hoped, however, that they might have them released by 22nd.

Even if that was the case, it was still cutting it very fine to get them collected, then flown from Rio to Porto Velho, and then from there to Crispinho.

It was the rainy season, and it was clear that it would be necessary to have some sort of cover for the service. The men set to and built a basic structure. A very large piece of orange plastic was flown in and with much heaving and pulling, was stretched out over the frame. This would at least keep the rain off. Some huge logs were assembled and planks of wood nailed to them to make improvised benches.

Food preparation was also being planned. Thirty one chickens and ten pigs would be needed. Rice and farinha would abound. The issue of drinking water was a problem. Shirley and Meinke were concerned that their visitors should not become ill through drinking contaminated water, as supplies of rain water were running low.

Lists were checked and double checked. Had they forgotten anything? Was everything ready? Well, apart from one vital box, everything else was as prepared as it could possibly be.

It was the day before the planned dedication when Shirley and Meinke stood on the edge of the airstrip waiting for the plane. So many memories had led them to this moment in history for the Paumarí. The children ran around excitedly. Other guests hovered in the background.

"Listen!" called one of the children. "Here it comes." There it was indeed as the little plane came into view and bumped along the airstrip. Everyone gathered round. And there it was! The precious box! Well, they certainly hoped that it was the right one.

There were plenty of willing hands to carry it to the improvised building.

At that time of the year it generally rained heavily at least once a day, often accompanied by fierce thunderstorms. Bad weather could severely restrict the incoming flights. Four flights a day were planned to bring in visitors and during the days when they started to arrive, there was no rain at all to cause disruption. However, by the evening of 23rd, supplies of drinking water were dangerously low.

That night it rained hard, very hard. It rained all night. So by morning there was plenty of water. As dawn broke, there was just drizzle in the air. A number of the visitors could be seen wandering around the muddy village muttering prayers. "Rain! Stop now!" Sure enough, the skies cleared and the sun broke through. Once again, God had proved His love and care for them, and had taken control, not only of the weather, but also of their need for relatively clean water.

Shirley and Meinke wondered how the Paumarí would react to so many different people coming to stay in the village, and especially the number of cameras and camcorders which would be pointed in their direction. In the event, however, the Paumarí rose to the occasion.

As the time approached for the service to begin, the precious box was carried to the front and placed on the table. It was still sealed. It certainly said 'Paumarí' on the outside, but would the contents really be correct? This was the moment.

After singing and prayers, Baiharo carefully slit open the box and gently lifted out the first red, soft bound New Testament! He turned it over slowly in his hands and then reverently lifted it high. Spontaneous clapping began, slowly at first and then reaching a great crescendo. Baiharo then handed a book to Totoi, and broad smiles filled their happy faces as they both held one up for their friends and family to see. As the applause ended, Totoi led in a prayer of thanksgiving.

It was a wonderful occasion. Surely the angels must have been singing. So many years of devoted work, so much love, so much commitment now presented in the precious word of God. It was the fulfilment of a dream.

The atmosphere was bubbling with excitement as Fátima and Zefina led the children in some singing. A number of the Paumarí had paid for a copy of the New Testament ahead of time. Some had made a small canoe or basket, while others had memorised certain passages of scripture. These now filed forward to receive their own copy as their names were called. Some of those who were active in leading the Paumarí church came forward to speak to their own people, and to encourage them to treasure the precious gift of God's word. Various visitors also came forward to bring greetings and encouragement.

As the service drew to a close, everyone streamed outside to enjoy a barbeque. Plates were filled with fish, chicken and pork as villagers and guests mingled together. Not another drop of rain fell until the last flight had left with all remaining guests. After that, the rainy season continued in its normal way.

In 1917, a young missionary named William Cameron Townsend was working with a group of people called the Cakchiquel, but was frustrated that they did not have the Bible in their own language. He caught the vision that every group of people, no matter how small or remote, should have the scriptures to read for themselves.

In response to his vision, he founded the Wycliffe Bible Translators and its sister organization, the Summer Institute of Linguistics. For over 50 years, these organizations have worked with others, united in the belief that God wants people to read His Word.

Way back in 1987 the Brazilian director of Wycliffe wrote an article. In it he said that if you counted all the New Testaments published by the mission and other colleagues since 1951, the average completed work was 7.3 per year. By 1961 it was 10 a year. By 1971 there was an average of 15.8 per year. By 1981 it was 22 per year. His article continued to say that in the previous five years a brand new, first time New Testament had been delivered to a language group somewhere in the world every 16 – 17 days.

Between 1999 and 2010 Wycliffe personnel have helped in the translation of more than 200 New Testaments and begun a new work in more than 670 languages.

What a remarkable achievement! Shirley's story is but one among so many lives which have been dedicated to God and the vision to translate His word. A few were called to make the ultimate sacrifice. It is God alone who knows the number of hours and tears which make up these statistics.

We honour individuals and organisations, wherever they may be and under whatever banner they work, in fulfilling this calling.

15 Full circle

Mind the Gap! Mind the Gap! As the London underground train rumbled and rattled through the tunnels of the capital, these words of warning had become familiar. At those stations where the platform was, of necessity, curved to follow the contour of the tunnel, there could be a significant gap between the train and the platform. Any unwary traveller could trip and break a leg or lose their valuables down the gap, hence the warning shouted by an anonymous voice over the loudspeaker system wherever there was a hazard.

Now back in England for retirement – whatever that was - Shirley thought about the words 'Mind the Gap!' and could not help but ponder the gap which existed between so many people in the world. There was an obvious gap between the rich and the poor, those who had enough of the basic necessities of life and those who did not, those who had the chance of education and those who did not. The list was endless.

Her mind wandered back to the early days of life with the Paumarí. If ever there was a group of people who could be classified as 'have nots', it was them. Way back then the gap between the villagers and more developed people had been huge. But over the years the gap had narrowed. Many of them could now read and do maths. They had some health workers, and two of their own who could pull teeth. They understood more about health and hygiene, and the Paumarí tribe had actually increased considerably in number from one hundred to around a thousand. Their children received some schooling. They had learned about money and had been paid with it for a long time. Most precious of all, they now had a sizeable chunk of the scriptures in their own language. They themselves had been part of the process, and those who had acted as language helpers had been invaluable. They had their own church with leaders from among their own people.

What would happen to the gap, she wondered, now that she had retired? Would they continue to follow the truths which they had learned in the Word of God? Would they succumb to the old temptations and go astray? Only time would tell.

For Shirley herself, she had a gap of her own to mind. She had not lived permanently in England for 35 years. There were plenty of gaps which she had to cross. Life in England was different. Even the currency had been decimalised, although she had experimented with the new coins on her occasional home visits.

But nearly everything was different. The culture had changed and even as she moved around the town there were so many languages being spoken which she did not recognise. She found that she could get on a bus and not hear English being spoken at all, and it was not unusual to be the only white person travelling on it. She was used to living in a different culture, but somehow this was all a bit alien.

Friends had changed. Some had moved away and others had died. Life-long friends would always remain as such, but in day to day life she needed to make new friends. With the best will in the world, they could not all share her heart for the Paumarí.

There were important decisions to make. Some of her local friends had become part of a new church set up and she had to decide where she would make her spiritual home. It was not a straightforward decision and she felt torn two ways.

Early on in her life with the Paumarí, she had grappled with the kinship system. As she had flown into the village on the first day so many years ago, she had wondered if she would ever be accepted by the people as their friend. They had certainly done that. They were more than friends. They had absorbed her into their family system and that had been a huge honour. She had become 'the other mother' to every baby which she had delivered. But she missed them all. They were as much a part of her as the blood relations she had in England.

The Paumarí had often said that when she and Meinke were out of the village, they felt like chicks without a mother. As they themselves had flown out, Meinke had gazed out of the window with misty eyes, saying that she felt like a mother hen with no chicks. They had mothered and nurtured these people, living with them through thick and thin, crises and dramas. Now there was a sense of bereavement. It was a break with the past.

Life in Porto Velho had also taken a sizeable chunk of her time, and as she reflected on her home and studies there, she realised that a considerable amount of her time in Brazil had been spent at the centre. Colleagues and members were also like family. She would miss them too. She and Meinke had lived and worked closely together for over twenty years, but that too was about to change.

Had she come home? Where was home? When she had first gone to South America, people had been aware of the challenges of adjusting to a new culture. In reality, coming back was equally demanding. The gap was huge. Where should she begin?

During those early months back in England, there were practical issues of getting her flat organised, and all the day to day necessities of banking and other administration. Bills and repairs seemed to need constant attention. As she tackled her garden, she realised that emotionally and spiritually, she had to replant her life and allow new roots to grow. It would take time.

She had been sure that God had guided her to come back to England. She was grateful that she had not made the decision lightly. Emotions caught her by surprise and she found that she would sit and weep by the hour. What for? She had absolutely no idea.

Having made the decision about which church to attend, there were still many adjustments to make. She had been with the Paumarí church right from its birth, and had been a leader and guide, teaching by word and example. In England, the leadership system was different, and she must adapt.

As some of the practical issues became more organised, there was the bigger question of 'What next?' She was not ready to pull on her slippers and rock in a chair!

As she thought about the transition both for the Paumarí and for herself, she began to consider ways in which she could maintain links with them. As she read some of the apostle Paul's letters again, she could identify with his longing to see friends from the various churches, and to encourage them. She was grateful that transport systems did make things easier for her than it was for Paul, although the journey to Brazil seemed to get longer every time she did it.

She thought of Paul with quill, papyrus and ink as he wrote his letters. Mastering all the idiosyncrasies of her computer nearly drove her crazy at times, but it was incredible to think how equipment had changed since the early days when she had gazed in horror at the mould growing daily on her battered typewriter.

There would always be plenty of jobs which she might do, and certainly could do. But what did God want her to do? It would be so easy to run around here and there being busy, busy, busy, but unless it was His calling for her, then it would be in vain. During the months of wondering what God had planned for her, Shirley often came back to a question. In her order of priorities, was there anything which she was able to do which no one else could? Her contact with the Paumarí ranked high on the list.

A request came from the village. Some of the Paumarí had seen the Jesus film in Portuguese, but were asking if it was possible to have it with Paumarí speech. Oh! What a challenge.

As Shirley and Meinke considered the project, they realised that if it was to happen, then they themselves would have to write the script. Almost immediately, they felt a huge weight of oppression. They had known similar attacks over the years and this was severe. The powers of darkness clearly did not want this idea to get off the ground.

In some ways, such spiritual opposition only strengthened their resolve to continue to reach out to the Paumarí. Both were agreed that they would take up the challenge. Plans were made for Shirley and Meinke to revisit the Paumarí village towards the end of 2004, and to stay for six weeks. In preparation for that they would both work on the script for the film, and needed to prepare between 40 – 60 selected readers from the village to take the speaking parts. Almost as an aside, Shirley planned to reorganise the Paumarí dictionary into a more user friendly format before she went. The Paumarí, however, wanted it in an alphabetical order, and this proved to be unworkable.

With an experienced technical support team in place, and a generator to power the equipment, one by one several Paumarí took their place behind the microphone to dub the film in their own language. What a momentous event.

As time went on, Shirley became involved with the Easy English [31] team, which had been devised by Wycliffe Associates. It was a translation from normal English to a very simplified form, designed for people with a limited grasp

[31] *www.easyenglish.info*

of the language. There were different levels and in some, an overall précis of the book also gave valuable insight as a Bible commentary. Some books had also been prepared for those with learning difficulties or limitations of speech. The early draft on the gospel of Mark in Paumarí had been one of Shirley's first attempts at translation. Now she found herself back in Mark's gospel with Easy English. Later on she became one of the Easy English coordinators.

From time to time news from the Paumarí brought smiles. Meinke reported on a bus journey which she had made with Baiharo. She had travelled with him to the graduation ceremony of Edilson. Meinke had discovered a side to Baiharo during that long journey which she had not seen in him before. At times he entertained the whole bus, and at other times he grasped the opportunity to have a captive audience.

"We are all evangelicals," he told the passengers. "We are following the Jesus road. Meinke is travelling with us. She taught us about God and helped to translate the Bible for us. We have our own church in the village now. Jesus gave us a new life and hope."

Not all his audience listened quietly. One lady challenged him, saying that the Paumarí should preserve their culture and customs. He was ready with a reply. "Every culture keeps changing the whole time, yours and ours. We want to have the right to choose what we want to change and what we want to keep. We know what isn't good for us. For this reason the decision should be ours."

"Good on you!" thought Shirley, as she could imagine the scene. How proud she was of him in defending the truth.

Other messages brought tears. Dosohani and his wife Raimunda had been expecting a baby, but Raimunda suffered a major haemorrhage following the birth, and had died. The baby was alive and well, but Dosohani was struggling with his grief. Shirley's heart ached for him.

Another letter reported that a young boy had drowned in the lake. Yet another, reported on the death from meningitis of Ernesto, the 12 year old son of Totoi and Gilsa. They were in a canoe taking him to Lábrea for medical help. Although in a coma, his consciousness returned for a brief moment just before he died. He lifted his head and said, "Mummy, Daddy, don't cry. I am seeing a beautiful place. I am going to be with Jesus. You will see me again."

Such news brought immense sadness as she thought of them struggling with their grief, whilst at the same time, trying to guide the church through their own sense of bereavement and questions. How she longed to be with them at these times.

Life in England was never boring. A pregnancy crisis centre was to be opened in the church, and Shirley offered to get involved. There were several weeks' training, and role play had her acting out some imaginary situations from village life! With the centre up and running, it provided a place of safety for women to come and discuss their personal situation. They could have a free pregnancy test, and depending on the result, considered the options open to them without the pressure of those who might have forceful opinions to thrust upon them. Most situations were complex and some were heartbreaking.

One letter which Shirley sent out to friends spoke of her own 'organ recital'. A nasty fall resulted in a broken elbow. She later needed a cholecystectomy to remove her gall bladder, but was amazed at the speed of recovery from the keyhole surgery compared with what she remembered from nursing days. An angiogram showed that one artery was 70% blocked, but for some while it was decided to leave well alone.

Later on another angiogram showed further blockage of the artery. A successful angioplasty was performed to insert a stent, although the surgeons found it technically difficult and sweated considerably for a couple of hours to get it in satisfactorily. The end result considerably improved her energy levels, and reduced the episodes of angina.

A number of Brazilians had been meeting in a local church and Shirley enjoyed her contact with them. Most of their services were in Portuguese, although they had one in English from time to time. She began to help some of them with their mastery of the English language, and in turn, was able to brush up on her own Portuguese. Sometimes she was invited to preach at their service and that sharpened her Portuguese even more. The leader of the group, Rogério Rosa da Silva, was particularly interested in the work with the Paumarí.

Rogério's UK visa had expired, and it was necessary for him to leave the country and return to Brazil. On one of her return visits, Shirley arranged to meet up with him, and for them to go with Meinke to the village. At the end of the visit, Rogério shared with them that he felt God's call to complete the translation of the Old Testament into Paumarí, which the villagers were asking for. He would need to do the necessary training, before returning to live in the village and learn the language. It was the answer to many years of prayer to God, that He would put a desire into Brazilians to share God's word with their indigenous neighbours.

There was also exciting news that a course designed for mother-tongue translators was to begin in Brazil. Three of the Paumarí hoped to go.

Such news reminded Shirley over and over again of the challenges in translating God's word into Paumarí. She recalled a conversation which she had with a language helper about stealing names. They had discussed whether it was possible to use the expression 'to ask in My name' in Paumarí. Previous attempts to do so had ended in failure. They had considered 'Jesus' name' and 'called Jesus', and agreed that they meant the same. But the language helper, Chico, had explained a problem. Someone had written a letter requesting fuel, and had used Chico's name at the end of the letter without his knowledge or consent.

"He stole my name," Chico said sadly. It led to a discussion about how easy it was to misuse the name of Jesus. Someone can use His name without the authority to do so, or fail to ask when God's provision is available. Either way, a vital relationship with Jesus is necessary.

The Paumarí had such a low opinion of themselves when Shirley first arrived to live with them, and lacked confidence to tackle many things. Over the years, those who had decided to follow the teachings of Jesus had begun to experience a new sense of self worth. They had started to appreciate who they were in Christ, and it was exciting that many of them did now know that they were part of God's family and, as such, had the privilege of using Jesus' name. But for all language helpers, be they mother-tongue translators, Brazilians or English speakers, there would always be challenges in providing not only an accurate translation, but also one which made sense in the culture.

This book has not retold half of the medical crises which Meinke suffered over the years. Any one of them might have killed her. However, more than 25 years on from Christmas 1985 when it seemed only a matter of hours before her life would slip away, Shirley and Meinke went on holiday together. Both continue to 'run the race' that is set before them, although perhaps at a slightly more sedate pace than before.

The letters which Shirley wrote to her father had been carefully preserved. Hundreds of them, on fragile airmail paper, have provided a most precious insight into the life and work of this remarkable lady. Her gracious, humble and dignified spirit are the bedrock of all she is. However, if I was to dare give her a polished halo, I know that there would be trouble!

In anything which I write, it is my deepest desire that God should get the glory. Shirley would want nothing less.

However, it is right that we honour her work and that of Mary Ann and Meinke who were alongside her for so many years. They would say that despite all the hardships of living in such a remote location, in spite of all the challenges, in spite of disappointments and through life-and-death crises, they would not have wanted to be anywhere else. They knew that they were where God wanted them to be. They knew His protection and strength on an hourly basis. It was God alone who brought them through.

The final words come from Paul's letter written to the church in Ephesus.

"Be prepared. You're up against far more than you can handle on your own. Take all the help you can get, every weapon God has issued, so that when it's all over but the shouting, you'll still be on your feet. Truth, righteousness, peace, faith and salvation are more than words. Learn how to apply them. You'll need them throughout your life. God's word is an indispensable weapon. In the same way, prayer is essential in this ongoing warfare. Pray hard and long. Pray for your brothers and sisters. Keep your eyes open. Keep each other's spirits up so that no one falls behind or drops out."

He concluded with a blessing. *"Good-bye friends. Love mixed with faith be yours from God the Father and from the Master, Jesus Christ. Pure grace and nothing but grace be with all who love our Master, Jesus Christ."* [32]

[32] *Ephesians 6: 13-18 and 23-24 (The Message)*

Dedication of the New Testament in Paumari